D0559460

# TOUGH NOTES:
## A HEALING CALL
## FOR CREATING EXCEPTIONAL
## BLACK MEN

# Books by Haki R. Madhubuti

# TOUGH NOTES:
## A HEALING CALL
## FOR CREATING EXCEPTIONAL
## BLACK MEN
### Affirmations, Meditations, Readings and Strategies

# Haki R. Madhubuti

**THIRD WORLD PRESS** Chicago

Third World Press
Publishers Since 1967
Chicago

First Edition
Printed in the United States of America

07 06 05 04 03 02  5 4 3 2
Cover design by Nicole Mitchell
Artwork by Jon Lockard
Photo by Lynda Koolish

Library of Congress Cataloging-in-Publication Data

Madhubuti, Haki R., 1942-
        Tough Notes:  A Healing Call for Creating
        Exceptional Black / by
Haki R. Madhubuti
        p. cm.
        ISBN:  0-88378-236-7 (alk. paper).
        1.

# DEDICATION

| | |
|---|---|
| Muhammad Ali | Fred L. Hord |
| Carl C. Bell | Bennett J. Johnson |
| Derrick Bell | John H. Johnson |
| Lerone Bennett Jr. | Malachi Favors Maghostut |
| Robert Bly | Walter Mosley |
| Avery Brooks | Dikembe Mutombo |
| Paul Coates | Useni E. Perkins |
| Jacob H. Carruthers | Sterling D. Plumpp |
| Noam Chomsky | Frank M. Reid III |
| William E. Cox | Studs Terkel |
| Ron Daniels | James Turner |
| Ossie Davis | Wesley Snipes |
| Howard Dodson | John Thompson |
| Leonard G. Dunston | Jeremiah A. Wright Jr. |
| Danny Glover | Quentin D. Young |
| | Howard Zinn |

*Men with large decencies in their hearts and for*

Margaret Burroughs        Barbara A. Sizemore

*Mentors and valiant examples*

# In Memoriam
**Gwendolyn Brooks**
**Dudley Randall**
**Paul Robeson**

**Glenn Thompson**

**Ralph Bunche**

**W.E.B. Dubois**

**Frantz Fanon**

**Calvin Hernton**

**Martin Luther King, Jr.**

**Darwin T. Turner**

**John Henrik Clarke**

**Claude Brown**

**Raymond R. Patterson**

**Howard Thurman**

**Margaret Walker**

# TABLE OF CONTENTS

# PREFACE

*Tough Notes: A Healing Call for Creating Exceptional Black Men,* a collection of essays unlike any of my other books of prose, is less technical and "bookish." These words are directed toward young men (and women) between the ages of fourteen and thirty-five. I am writing to my sons, cultural sons and young men wandering this land without a clue to its complexities and the many traps awaiting them. This book is for fatherless young people who wonder what a daddy is. I write for young men who must navigate the many options of right and wrong that they must face daily, and the millions of young brothers (Black, brown, white and others) who are caught like stray dogs in this very complicated economic, political and legal system. The jails and prisons across this land that they populate like second homes is a national shame and should be an embarrassment to all freedom loving people.

These essays are for non-readers, slow readers and those who read one thousand words a minute. They are in the form of essays, notes and one page ideas. Some of the subjects like Anti-Rape, Fathering, Children, Black Women, Reading and History I have visited before in my other works. The idea for *Tough Notes* came to me after spending over thirty-nine years in very active community work, and from my involvement in the building of independent Black schools and institutions in Chicago. After the publication of *Black Men: Obsolete, Single, Dangerous?* in 1991, I received thousands of letters and calls from young men requesting direction and mentoring. However, the most pressing reason for *Tough Notes* is my personal response to the hundreds of letters, notes and telephone calls I have received over the years from prisoners and students—mainly young Black men (many without caring or existing fathers), seeking guidance and a kind word. This work is for them and other young men and women systematically locked out of this nation's wealth, benefits and opportunities.

Of course, *Tough Notes* can be read by anyone of any culture, most certainly women and older men are encouraged to read it. However, my thoughts on most days are about young people, especially young Black and brown men, teenagers and boys, who populate the corners as discussed in the thousands of paragraphs printed in newspapers, magazines, books and dissertations claiming authority about their young lives.

My love for young people has a history, my own and that of the Black struggle in America. My love for young people has guided my writing, my work and life over the last thirty-nine years. At the confirming age of fifty-nine I feel more certain than ever that this can be a better world if all cultures were more child and youth-centered. The main ingredient that is missing in the lives of many young people (troubled and those doing "well") in the West is deep love, secure living and learning environments, progressive education and an "equal" chance to achieve and shine.

Increasingly, what is missing in their young lives is an informed introduction to the arts. Most young people have not been properly introduced to the developmental properties of art. When you look at the best schools in the land and the most nurturing homes and communities in the nation, the use of art instruction in all of its manifestations is clearly central to the education and enjoyment of its young. Art can heal, develop, inform, shape unknown possibilities and help confirm one's worth in a difficult world. Art allows caring teachers and parents a way to nurture and/or discover those inborn or undeveloped talents that most children have in music, dance, writing, acting, painting, photography, etc. Art is the window into understanding culture and our culture defines us. To that end, as a poet I do slip in a few poems to help bring clarity to a topic.

In keeping with the values articulated in *Tough Notes*, the book is priced close to what it cost to produce it. It will be discounted to youth-oriented social agencies and institutions that buy in bulk and in some cases donated to men and women in prisons, jails, boot camps, orphanages and foster homes.

This book is possible, in part, due to the help, advice, work and caring of the following persons: Safisha Madhubuti, Rose Perkins, Gwendolyn Mitchell, Bakari Kitwana, Nicole Mitchell, Melissa Moore, Bennett J. Johnson, Pamela York, and the students, English faculty and adminstrations of Chicago State University. And, of course, many thanks to my children.

As always, Love and More.


Haki R. Madhubuti

# A Poet's Call

it has always been easy
to get to my heart.
there is no other way of stating it.
the best poets are lovers,
are receptacles for pain, joy, injustice
and the innocent smiles of children.
we trust too early and easily,
we read potential in the countless faces of evil,
we carry many, many wounds
we are often crippled yet some heal quickly
only to open their hearts to stories our
       children can see through.
the right words can send us on unlimited journeys.
the hurt in chidren's eyes releases fury
       in our souls and fists,
Black girls' mistreated hair bring tears.
I do not wish it to always be this way
to care too much can damage one's spirit yet,
the secret to the longevity of significant poets is:
we never give up on love, poetry and
the smiles of the young.

# I.
## EMPOWERING THE SELF

An erosion of self-esteem is one of the
commonist symptoms of dispossession.
> —Chinua Achebe
> *Home and Exile*

It is the same spirit. The spirit of poor
people who have been ground down
nearly to a fine powder of humanity and
yet who stand like rocks and refuse to be
blown away.
> —Alice Walker
> *Living by the Word*

# WHO AM I?

If the question "Who am I?" is answered within a historical, political, economic, social and cultural context by Black people or people of African ancestry, also known as African Americans, early and often, there would be less confusion about Black identity, purpose, potential and one's place in a highly nationalistic and multicultural world. Having studied this question over the last three decades, I've concluded that we, the people the color of night, deep oak, coal, rich earth and the many colors in-between, have been taught and forced to define ourselves from the condition of the negative or as simply the opposite of white.

Blackness or one's Africaness, when interpreted by persons without a serious cultural education, is generally limited to one's personal struggles for day-to-day survival, this tends to be the anti of what one is struggling against. Therefore, to be Black too often in the West is to be a victim. As such, one is always responding to anti-Black racism, i.e., white supremacy. A person's Blackness or color is very seldom a positive affirmation of a whole self. In America, it is mostly limited to the generalities of Black peoples' popular culture. This includes a wide variety of things from the food we eat and the religion we practice, to the politics we espouse, the clothes we wear, as well as our dance, music, hair and language. Black popular culture (as portrayed in current popular

"Black" television shows) in addition to the businesses Blacks control (from beauty and barber shops, bars and liquor stores, to the thriving underground economy) are also part of what many of us erroneously use to define our Blackness. When all of this fails, some still rely on simplistic assertion, "I know what being Black is; I've been Black all of my life."

The problem with the popular culture approach to clarity is that there may be partial truth here, but it often dismisses the absolute necessity for serious and in-depth study of Black-African origins and culture. The real question is, "Who am I as an African American in relationship to American popular culture and America in general?" I think that we must first understand the gravity of the question. It is a question that at some point all people, regardless of ethnicity or culture, ask themselves. The answers have helped America's other racial and ethnic groups to position themselves within America.

As individuals of other ethnic groups confront the question, their answers may come easier because their cultures are more stable, institutionalized and empowered. As the English, Irish, Italian, Polish, Jewish, Chinese, and German and other Americans solidified their political and economic place in the United States, they built secular and sacred institutions that spoke directly to the cultural strengths, needs and desires of each group. Most members of America's other cultures are descendants of planned migrations who willingly came to the United States seeking a better life; whereas

Africans had no choice in the matter.

Up until the late twentieth century, most people of African ancestry in the United States were the descendants of people who had been enslaved by Europeans and European-Americans. We were forced into a new existence, acculturated into a slave and Euro-American reality, and ultimately redefined by human traders and human owners. African Americans are in this country because of race, and over the last three centuries our socialization in the United States has been based upon race. For the last three hundred and fifty years or so, most Black folks have been reacting to and struggling against the people, culture and condition of whiteness and Europe. A testament to this can be found in all aspects of American culture, including the language itself. In this dialectic anything Black (and most certainly the people with Black skin) is defined by Euro-American culture almost to a syllable as the opposite of white: negative, evil, lowdown, soiled, dismal, hostile, not hopeful, disastrous, wicked, ugly, untrustworthy, and ignorant.

The culture and systems of white supremacy have rendered most Black people politically and economically powerless, and often not credible even in something as fundamental as self-definition; hence the most recognizable and accepted authorities on Black people in the United States are non-Blacks. By contrast, to be white is validated and celebrated within American culture each day in thousands of ways. The great poet Gwendolyn Brooks writes clearly about whiteness in her essay

"Requiem Before Revival":

> I give whites big credit. They have never tried to be
> anything but what they are. They have been and will
> be everlastingly proud proud proud to be white. It
> has never occurred to them that there has been or
> ever will be ANYthing better than, nor one zillionth
> as good as, being white. They have an overwhelm-
> ing belief in their validity. Not in their "virtue," for
> they are shrewdly capable of a very cold view of
> that. But their validity they salute with an amazing
> innocence-yes, a genuine innocence, the brass of
> which befuddles most of the rest of us in the world
> because we have allowed ourselves to be hypno-
> tized by its shine.

A part of our answering the question "Who am I?"
must come from the thoughtful study of the history, politics, religion, sociology, psychology, literature, economics and culture of Black people. However, unlike
America's other ethic groups, African Americans for the
most part cannot point to a specific nation on the vast
continent of Africa and unequivocally claim it as the specific country of origin. This is part of our dilemma. The
search for the solution has driven many Blacks to "make
up stuff" as they are confronted with questions of identity. Some have adopted certain nations in Africa that they
believe are progressive and receptive to African
Americans. Others just claim all of Africa south of the

Sahara and try to incorporate into their lives the best of all of the hundreds of different and distinct ethnic and national groups. Refusing to join in the many African ethnic wars, the connection to Africa and Africans for those persons is not ethnic based. They claim all of Black Africa. They define themselves in the affirmative by incorporating into their lives the "best" of African cultures as they understand and interpret them. Of course, this is a difficult task and requires deep study and travel throughout Africa.

Regardless of their approach, most of these Black people are clearly American patriots. As African Americans they understand as W.E.B. DuBois articulated close to a hundred years ago that we are people of a dual consciousness in a "dark body," both African and American, fighting for meaning and acceptance. As American patriots, our people have always been in the forefront of the fight for freedom, democracy and inclusion into the mainstream of American life.

The Black Arts Movement (BAM) of the 1960s and 1970s went on the offensive and clearly accepted Africa as its starting point. For the poets, writers, visual artists and musicians of BAM, Black and Africa are synonymous. For most of them to be Black meant more than just one's color, but also spoke to one's culture, consciousness, potential and progressive tomorrows. This is why most of the BAM artists capitalized the word "Black" when used in reference to African people. Again to quote Ms. Brooks as she ponders this issue:

We still need the essential Black statement of defense and definition. Of course, we are happiest when that statement is not dulled by assimilationist urges, secret or overt. However, there is in "the souls of Black Folk"—even when inarticulate and crippled—a yearning toward Black validation.

To be Black is rich, is subtle, is nourishing and a nutrient in the universe. What could be nourishing about aiming against your nature?...

I continue my old optimism. In spite of all the disappointment and disillusionment and befuddlement out there, I go on believing that the Weak among us will, finally, perceive the impressiveness of our numbers, perceive the quality and legitimacy of our essence, and take sufficient, indicated steps toward definition, clarification.

If our struggles of the 1960s and 1970s taught us anything, it was the necessity of taking control of something as personal and fundamental as self-definition. Our great historians and educators—such as Carter G. Woodson, Vincent Harding, Chancellor Williams, John Henrik Clarke, Lerone Bennett Jr., Barbara A. Sizemore, John Hope Franklin, Darlene Clark Hine and hundreds of others who have devoted their lives to informing the world about the beauty and substance of Black folks— make it clear that we must be pro-active when it comes to accurately defining ourselves. At the same time, we must be careful not to buy into the feel good history of Black superiority and Black myth-making, but become searchers for the unvarnished truth. From the explosion of Black literature that has been published over the last thirty years, the national development of Black institutions (museums, publishing companies, book stores, schools, theaters, recording and film companies, banks and mega churches) to the continued revolution in Black music and the visual graphics of Black artists, photographers and film makers that are now commonplace, I would say we are on the right track.

Who am I? Try this: African Americans are the music of Louis Armstrong, James Brown, Duke Ellington, Billie Holiday, Aretha Franklin and Erykah Badu. We adhere to the spiritual ideas of the Bible, Koran, Torah and other holy texts as understood and interpreted by great Black preachers and ourselves. Our literature includes the works of Toni Morrison, Melvin B. Tolson, Terry McMillan, Robert Hayden, Walter Mosley and Octavia Butler. We are the dance of Alvin Ailey, Dance Theatre of Harlem and Muntu Dance Theatre. When it comes to language and speech, we reflect the works of Geneva Smitherman, Frank M. Reid III, Cornel West, Clarence Page, Julianne Malveaux and Johnetta B. Cole. Our focus on education includes the approaches of Edgar Epps, Barbara Sizemore, Carol D. Lee, James Anderson, historically Black colleges and universities, and much more. Black economics extend from the three billion dollar sellout of BET, the family-owned Johnson Publishing Company to the tens of millions of working Black women, men and young people. Black politics are the Congressional Black Caucus, state legislators and urban centers and the ideas of Ronald Walters, bell hooks, Ron Daniels, Manning Marable, Frances Beale, Angela Davis, and millions of others. Our food consists of southern cooking, fresh vegetables from home gardens and fresh fruit and vegetable juices. Our sports include the Williams sisters, NBA, WNBA, and the cold reality that if given an equal playing field in all areas of life we will excel. We are truly America's metaphor for its best citizens and the most misunderstood people in this great land.

However we can no longer accept ignorance as an excuse for a lack of cultural awareness. The "who" is in the "I" that all of us must answer each day. It is the responsibility of each of us to do the necessary work of educating ourselves and informing our extended family about the great possibilities of life. If we do anything less than love ourselves, make the right connections to each other, understand the complexities that we face and prepare for all possibilities we, by definition, will not graduate from victim-hood to ownership of ourselves and the coming worlds.

Am I overly optimistic? I doubt it. If history is our guide, it is clear that we have survived the hurricanes and volcanoes that others have thrown against us. It is now our own fires that must be controlled, understood, organized and made ready to confront and conquer whatever awaits us. The only certainty in this journey is that this will be our most difficult of struggles. The doors have cracked open, but sliding through is not acceptable. Being confused about who we are only leads to more confusion, and that too, in this new millennium, is not acceptable.

# A Call to Men

We are living in very difficult and tumultuous times. Ethnic and religious "cleansing" is sweeping much of the world with belated responses from responsible and caring people. Armed children are murdering other children as if they are part of some omnipresent video game. The nation's prison population is approaching two million. The vast majority of these inmates are young Black, Latino and poor White men. The drug culture plays a large part in the warehousing of young people. All over the nation, many Black men and boys are in psychological and spiritual conflict as a result of the culture of violence, drugs and prison that is the only America they know. What kind of civilization would allow for such a gigantic disruption of its young?

In our search for solutions, how will Black men and boys prepare themselves for the twenty-first century and beyond? How do we define the new Black man, the man of African ancestry or the "African American" man in today's politically charged climate? What approaches to life will be most effective for developing a new leadership among us who are visionary, talented, spiritually grounded and incorruptible individuals? How do young Black men institute a healing culture of fairness, love, and respect in personal relationships? What role does religion and spirituality play in our lives, and how will it prepare us for the challenges ahead? How do young

Black men prepare themselves for the new technologies and economics of the West? Finally, how do young Black men celebrate themselves, maintain a wholistic and healthy approach to life, while living in a highly combative, complicated, racist and confused world? These issues require deep reflection, discussion, and the application of life-giving and life-saving tools for personal empowerment. By this I mean life giving strategies that are both practical and applicable to the lives of everyday people. Such strategies will encourage and direct them to be better than they and others expect them to become. Many of the ideas and suggestions stressed within are based upon my own maturation, the observations of others, serious study, much national and international travel and work in the many communities of the Black world.

However, all Black men must give the deepest thought and action to personal and professional relationships, especialy those with women, children and family. At all times, Black men need to think and evaluate where they are as men, co-workers, lovers, husbands, fathers and brothers in a healthy and developmental manner. This requires work, serious study and a profound commitment to quality relationships at all levels of human interaction.

All of my reflections throughout this book have a common theme—the making of exceptional men. To this end, many of the essays question where we are, where we are going and where I think we must be. My view of the state of Black people in the United States is not a self-righteous one, but an analysis based upon close to forty years of active political and cultural struggle, much study, teaching, institution building and deep contemplation on our enduring battle with the multiple forces of economics, politics, education, Euro-centralism, media, and health care. All of these are rigged rather quietly in the philosophy of white world nationalism that perpetuates and legitimizes itself in institutions like the World Bank, International Monetary Fund, world media, urban school systems and the corporate rulership of the West.

I realize that I do not have the final say on any of this. I am a poet who quite early in my journey recognized that I needed to do much more than write, read and study poetry. My life's work has been a small river in the struggle for the liberation of people of African ancestry and others. This commitment has been very costly, emotionally, spiritually and monetarily. I am not alone in understanding the price of liberation. Few who chose this work survive in a healthy state.

We, Black men, must understand that we are particularly negated in a world run by men, and in our case in the United States, white men. Black men and women have been fighting multiple wars since our forced migration to this land, and our current condition is the most telling example of our confused existence and total dependence on a system and people who care little if anything (other than that which is negative) about us.

This book is a call for young brothers and Black men to stand tall and bold, to develop and deliver—if not for ourselves, most certainly for our children and their future.

# Men Among Us

My brothers, there are exceptional men among us. Men who took their young years, most against great odds, to prepare themselves to be the best in their chosen fields. Most of these men understood early how racism / white supremacy worked and therefore resisted its traps and temptations and fortified their bodies, minds and spirits to rise against its evils. These men are in the tradition of Martin Delaney, W.E.B. DuBois, Paul Robeson, Malcolm X, John Coltrane, Arthur Ashe, Romare Bearden, Thurgood Marshall, A.G. Gaston, Marcus Garvey, Martin Luther King Jr. and others. Exceptional men, known and unknown, are many among us. Some of them are your fathers, grandfathers, uncles, teachers, ministers, coaches, friends and mentors.

Being a man of African ancestry, a Black man in America, for most of us has been like pushing a plow in a dry field without a horse or mule. Most often, we have had to navigate life through the worldview, ideas, culture, systems and prejudices of others that has forced many of us into mediocrity, a blinding hopelessness and destroyed a good percentage of us. Being born Black, male and developing into Black manhood is often, in America, a dangerously paralyzing journey. Because of the dangers and the many traps set to steer Black boys away from being responsible men, it is critical that you understand that being a man is not just a function of biology. Just as important are culture, community values, current knowledge base, spiritual connectedness, positive self-concept, family relationships, friendships, brotherhood, work and a work ethic, health, loveships, a winning and creative attitude toward life, intelligence and a willingness to learn, grow and change when necessary.

Many Black men have missing moments in their lives. Many of these moments have to do with our fathers or the absence of a father. Often the pain of being fatherless is deep and requires much work to bridge the conflicts felt within. Men seldom talk about their problems to others. We too often let problems build up in us until they boil over and burst loudly in inappropriate, often hurting and embarrassing ways. The projected image of what a man is or should be in this culture is often at odds with being a whole, mature and loving person. This is manifested in the way we relate to women, the way we raise our children, educate ourselves and how we approach the personal and public world of work and play. Whether you are fathers or not, you must learn how to keep effectively growing in a loving way. This is not an easy journey and requires you to commit yourself to the following:

1. Have regular conversations with someone you trust, preferably an older man—father, grandfather, uncle or close male friend.
2. Participate in activities that build self esteem, such as

improving upon your education, part-time school, evenings, weekends or a combination of both; if you have a high school education, consider community colleges, probaby the most democratic institution of higher education.

3. Work in an area that gives you satisfaction, joy and brings out the best in you.

4. Nurture relationships that are understanding, loving and special.

5. Find a new environment—a new community that can aid and stimulate the growth potential in you

6. Maintain a frame of mind that insists that you are not a victim but an adult experiencing temporary problems that you can fix.

7. Listen to your own life-affirming spirit and locate a spiritual and faith community that compliments your own words and needs

8. Exercise and eat properly—keep your weight down and stay in shape—if you look good and feel good about yourself, you will radiate a positive aura.

9. Study, study, study—the more you understand the intricacies of life—personal and public—the better you will be able to handle most things that come before you. Consider making the public library a regular stop during your week. An active library card is a must for people seeking to build their minds with current and up to date information and knowledge.

Most exceptional men understand and incorporate the lessons of history in their lives. We are here because strong men and women preceeded us and created the paths we now tread upon. We are not without examples, contemporary and historical, that offer bright direction. Look closely in your immediate communities. Don't forget your own family. There are thousands of men who are all around us, wanting to be asked for help.

# Spirituality,
# Practicing Faith

Weekly in America, Black people by the millions fill churches, mosques, synagogues and temples of worship. During the historic Million Man March over eighty-five percent of the men attending were Christians and deep believers. Upon being interviewed after winning an event, most Black athletes' initial response is to thank God for their performance. Most Black actors and entertainers receiving Emmys or other awards keep God at the center of their acceptance comments. Throughout the Black world, faith is at the epicenter of most Black communities and cultures. There are many remarkable characteristics common to Black people, but the one constant that seems to be universal is our undeniable and all embracing acceptance of and belief in God.

The universality of Black faith, whether Christian, Muslim, Jewish, Yoruba, Hindu, Akan, Buddhist, etc., is an important variable in the core identity of people of African ancestry. Most believe that there is an entity greater than human, animal, or insect responsible for all existence. In general, this entity is deemed "God" and is all good, all knowing and all powerful. This God is complex, loving and fair. In good times and bad times, "God" will be there for you. The thinking and belief goes, if you commit yourself to deep prayer and meditation, read and study the sacred books, practice the messages of God's holy words, live a moral, ethical and productive life, do good towards all and live with unconditional love in your heart; you will be rewarded in your current and next life. This is extremely difficult in a world that worships the rich and decadent, exalts the most outrageous, and miserably fails to protect its children, elderly and poor.

Nothing better illustrates the challenge of practicing faith in today's world than the contemporary scene of Black ministers. A significant number of Black preachers and ministers today are into the ministry of prosperity and celebrity. In this arena, out and out greed clouds the reality of the gospel. Often, the religious leader's personal lifestyle is more in line with that of Bob Johnson or Donald Trump rather than Jesus Christ. Their yearly contributions to Germany and Japan in the purchase of Mercedes and Lexus cars has the great theologian Howard Thurman turning in his grave.

I'm clearly against poverty for any people, and most certainly I believe that one's spiritual and secular leadership should live in a manner that allows them to maximize their work and message. However, such a lifestyle should not be contradictory to their message, nor should they make deals with the devil in the name of short term personal or massive gains for themselves or their chosen people. Today we are surrounded by preachers as celebrities—known for being known. Pop-up preachers who are there when the television cameras arrive and/or pay for cable time each week to broadcast their message.

Preachers as celebrities are nothing new. We have a

history of this in the Black community from Father Divine and Daddy Grace to Reverend Ike and Reverend Henry Lyons. What is needed is a gospel of liberation based on everybody being spiritually rich rather than a serious call to live a materially backward life in concert with the most decadent of the world's rulership. In this world, there will always be serious disparities between the haves and the have-nots. However, for good people, regardless of wealth or religion, the necessary call is to work incessantly for the greater good for the majority of the world's people rather than the elite or "chosen" few.

As a child and as an adult I have witnessed well-known African American men of "God" in their ugliest and most un-Godly ways. One of the most powerful Baptist ministers in the country, a former head of the National Baptist Convention, used my mother as his personal mistress in the early 1950s. At the time, my sister, my mother and I occupied the basement apartment of a building he owned. His warped demands on her went far beyond her role as the building's janitor.

However, during the day he was the pillar of his community. On Sundays, he preached the "message" like few others could. He was truly blessed with riches, the love of his congregation and his family. My mother was his "outside" woman and she cleaned his apartment building as if our lives depended on it. I'll never forget her carrying garbage cans three flights to the ground each week, mopping the halls and back porch twice a week and much, much more. We lived there until he

tired of her and his wife finally could not stand it anymore. We were put out, never to hear from him or her
again until his untimely and unexpected death.

As an adult I have witnessed some of the nation's
most powerful men of faith act as if they truly answer to
no one, not even God. Some of them, after building
churches of ten, twelve and twenty thousand live personal lives that were/are decadent and hypocritical in the
extreme. And yes, their assistants, spokespersons,
women and men parishioners make all kinds of excuses
for them—even as they, themselves know deep in their
souls the sinful, ungrateful, selfish and hypocritical lives
their leaders live. The most recent national example of
this in the Black community is the Rev. Henry Lyons of
St. Petersburg, Florida. He abused his faith and his offi-
cial office and is now serving time in prison.

Billions of people daily surrender their lives to the
power of faith, redemption, love, forgiveness, reciprocity, service, sharing and trust in God(s). But if we put too
much faith in the "faith bringer," the "earthly voice of
God," we may be betrayed and could spend a lifetime
running from house of worship to house of worship,
from faith bringer to faith interpreter, to sheep in wolf's
clothing, be they tailor-made. Everyone, even in the
warm arms of one's belief system, must take personal
responsibility. Indeed, we are social and communal in
our faith. Yet, we remain thinking individuals. And,
even though it is much easier to believe than think, you
will experience less disappointment and pain in your

heart if you try critical thinking as you seek faith and deep understanding in a secular, empirical and commercial world.

The capacity of man to do unspeakable harm is on display daily. Warning: If a minister dressed in tailor-made suits, dark glasses and designer shoes shows up with bodyguards, a large entourage and a message about the living God that rivals the productions of James Brown, watch out! Hold on to your wallets and minds. If you are to become one with God and yourself, unselfish acts of goodness, love, sharing, compassion, thinking, meditating, good work/labor and prayer must be at the center of your life. In the final analysis, it doesn't matter what faith you practice. It is the practice that reveals the true position of the heart, spirit, soul and mind.

The best test of one's faith is the formal and informed study of other faith traditions. I am very serious about this. Too often believers claim the righteousness and universality of their faith without ever leaving the comfortable confines of one's church, temple, synagogue or place of worship. If indeed one is on the "correct path" to enlightenment, most certainly the in-depth study of other faith traditions can only add to one's understanding of the religious world and one's own spiritual place in it. Remember, God speaks in more than one language.

If a believer—it doesn't matter what religion or spiritual path—adds selective travel into other faith-based cultures, that is, walks among them, listens to and engages in conversation with them, then this will only bring deeper clarity to the believer's own tradition. Such study and travel will also facilitate new and complex questions for which the truly faithful, if indeed they are spiritually committed, must seek answers in their own traditions.

Beware of spiritual leaders who loudly and unequivocally proclaim that he or she has the "only way." The one way message in a world as large (six billion people) and as diverse as this one, is rather naive, ignorant or a downright con game. Spiritual differences exist from nation to nation, from culture to culture at the same level, or at a greater level than politics, economics and diets.

Finally, I do believe that spiritual growth, spiritual commitment and a spiritual life-style are essential in forging peace and well being among people in the world. However, if this requires our undying commitment to a faith tradition that necessitates our joining "righteous" campaigns against the so-called infidels or unbelievers, we will never rid ourselves of one of the major causes of death, poverty and natural displacement—*religious war*.

# Lest We Forget

What will the new century bring us? How will we walk our talk? What will we do when it is revealed that the "dot com" revolution has more holes in it than natural sponges and is much less dependable? If indeed there is a healing spirit in this universe, how will it reorder our secular notions of love, especially the love between people of different cultures and races? Actually, what use is MTV, BET, the major networks and all other cutting edge media if they do not seriously address man's inhumanity to children, animals, the environment and each other? And, who is truly educated and what is the ultimate test of a quality education when over the last sixty years or so the "civilized" world has allowed genocide after genocide?

Two recent books have again prompted me to visit the pessimistic side of my brain. *We Wish To Inform You That Tomorrow We Will Be Killed With Our Families* by Philip Gourevitch and *Neighbors* by Jan Tomasz Gross are works that demand that we continuously consider the moral and ethical side of the human condition. In *We Wish To Inform You That Tomorrow We Will Be Killed With Our Families*, a title that accurately defines its content, Gourevitch gives us the gut-wrenching tales from the 1994 genocide where the Rwandan government called on its Hutu majority to systematically carry out a "program of massacres" that killed over 800,000 Tutsi people—men, women, children and the unborn still in their mother's wombs.

For the geographically challenged, Rwanda is a small nation in central east Africa, bordering Uganda on the north and Burundi and Tanzania on the south, the democratic Republic of the Congo (formerly Zaire) is to its immediate west and Kenya is just across Lake Victoria to its northeast. Rwanda, like most of Africa's nation states, is a European construct with a long and recent history of European colonialism. Upon independence, Rwanda, like most of post-colonial Africa, maintained strong religious and governmental connections to Europe. The main ethnic groups who live there are the Hutu majority and the Tutsi minority.

Gourevitch's insights into the genocide (as defined by the United Nations) of the Tutsi people and its aftermath, which was allowed to run its course for over a hundred days in the spring and summer of 1994, clearly remind us of the long distances we still have to travel before we can truly call ourselves civilized human beings. Likewise, Jimmy Briggs' reports from Rwanda that appeared in *The Source* (August 1999) and *Choices* (August 1999) were equally critical, especially his concentration on Rwanda's children. Mr. Briggs reports on an evil that literally took children and made them kill their own family members. Briggs carefully considers the long lasting trauma of such cruel and inhuman acts. The shameful non-response of Kofi Annan and the United Nations and Bill Clinton and humanitarian forces of the United States should never be forgotten if this is not to happen again. The lessons of Rwanda are many, but for me it was the latest and loudest indication that a part of Africa is losing its soul. All people, of all cultures and races, are capable of enormous evil in the name of nationalism, religion or ethnic identity.

Which brings me to *Neighbors* by Jan Tomasz Gross, a Jewish-born native of Poland who now resides in New York and teaches at New York University. Mr. Gross writes of a little-known massacre during the German initiated eradication of Europe's Jewish population, now known as the Holocaust. His eye is on his homeland Poland, which he left after the anti-Semitic propaganda campaigns of the late 1960s. Mr. Gross updates the historical record in the farming village of Jedwabne, Poland where on July 10, 1941 Polish citizens, under the watchful eyes of German soldiers, rounded up 1,600 Jedwabne Jewish men, women and children in the town square, beat and stoned them, crowded them into a barn like animals, locked it and set it on fire, burning the Jewish people to death.

The historical myth is that the massacre of Jews on that fateful day was the work of the Gestapo and Nazi soldiers. In fact there was a stone monument in Jedwabne that stated in no uncertain terms, "Site of a massacre of Jews, Gestapo and Nazi soldiers burned 1,600 people."* However, it is Mr. Gross' research, interviews and deep investigation that shock the local population who for over fifty-seven years were unaware that it was the neighbors of the Jews who designed and carried out mass murder of 1,600 fellow Polish citizens who happened to be Jews.

Whether in Rwanda in the last decade of the twentieth century or Poland nearly sixty years ago, the message in both of these books is that we have not grown up. That the healing spirit that defines advanced civilizations is not a universal fact. When nations do not protect its minority populations, none of us are safe. When the members of the United Nations ignore the call of "little people" and the world community responds half-heartedly to the planned annihilation of defenseless people, none of us have the luxury of isolated thought and actions. Each of us in our hearts, spirits and actions must become mini United Nations of one; we must be willing to share from the depths of our souls the call of love and continued respect and support for all people, especially those minorities who find themselves trapped in the hands of evil men and women.

---

\* As a result of Jan Tomasz Gross' book *Neighbors*, this inaccurate Holocaust monument was removed on March 15, 2001. According to an article in the *Chicago Tribune,* "Jedwabne Mayor Krzyszt of Godlewski said the new monument's inscription should contain reflection and thoughtful consideration of history." Mr. Gross deserves a  strong hand of support for proving once again that books matter. This Jewish pogrom, one of the worst in Poland during World War II, will now be properly acknowledged.

# MONEY:
## Life Has Hard Calls

There is endless truth in the cliché "life is short." Like tears in the ocean or leaves in an autumn forest, measuring one's life span is like trying to count the stars of the galaxy in one second. Most of the world's population lives on average about forty-five years. People in the West, through advances in hygiene, education, wealth accumulation, technology and agriculture have rounded that number to about seventy-nine years. Still, life is a series of graduations from one level to the next, finally to arrive at adulthood where you are responsible for your own choices, decisions and actions in an unfair world. Yes, this world is not fair, safe or innocent for the majority of the world's inhabitants.

Most of the world's people spend the majority of their waking hours working. Generally they labor in the production of food, clothing, livable housing and clean water. Serious leisure time does not exist for the working poor who over populate Asia, Africa, Eastern Europe, South and Central America. This is not to dismiss that the majority of people in the United States also have hard calls to make. For the first time in the history of this small planet, we live in a highly commercial and consumer driven society. The toys of western capitalism are available to all if they are able to buy outright, acquire credit cards or go the lay-away route. Television has transformed how many people view reality, that is those who control the air waves (radio included) construct alternate realities. Due to highly effective commericals, the engine that drives programming, we are taught to view debt acculumulation as an act of becoming an adult.

Most of us are not taught from birth to be frugal. Few of us save or do any serious investment. We live from paycheck to paycheck, and our knowledge of how this economy works is minimum at best. High school and college students are sent unsolicited credit cards. Many of them, before they're twenty years old, are experiencing debt. The new slavery is credit with its compound interest, which can legally be as high as thirty percent. This is truly non-discriminating. One of the most adult acts that you can participate in is taking control of your economic life. The hardest call is to say "no" to the easy, the quick, the sure fire, the "get it for nothing" attitudes. Everything has a price and most of us cannot afford it.

To measure your needs by that which is projected via mass media is a mistake that has no mercy. The average person views a minimum of one thousand advertisements a day. What used to be called "keeping up with the Joneses" is now keeping up with the world wide web or cyberspace. To spend in these contexts has no limits. To say "no" to the most outrageous commercials is an act of responsibility that needs to be taught early and often.

To live and build a life upon responsible learning and production rather than childish consumption and waste is very difficult in the United States and much of the Western world. Part of the problem is the pace of the this culture, the speed in which everything has to be done—from lovemaking to the rearing of children. We have bought into a mentality of quickness, fast for fast's sake, and the necessity of having it now. Federal Express, fax machines, and e-mail have replaced conversations, letter writing, smiles and hugs and storytelling at bedtime. The real crime is in the hypocrisy of leaders—private and public—who live as if "we the people" work for them. Michael Parenti, in his insightful book *America Besieged* writes:

> The real name of their (this) system is plutocracy, ruled by the wealthy few, the very opposite of democracy. In the interest of liberty and social justice, it should be hated and fought, resisted and replaced with a system of communal ownership and rigorous democratic protection for public and private well-being.

The hard call is to measure your own pulse; to meditate on the actual needs of your soul, spirit, mind and body; to understand quality and be opposed to the weakening quantity of mass production; to nurture family and friends; to seek relationships that are not oppressive but calming and caring, quiet and compatible to the windows of your eyes; to enjoy the simplicity of life: walking, experiencing nature, listening to and making music, reading the books you promised yourself, taking the classes so often put off, frequenting museums, libraries and visiting art, book and music festivals. Seek love and give it whenever possible, especially to children.

If you carry big debt, spend wildly as if there is no tomorrow, work two or more jobs just to pay everybody and their momma off, you have willfully forfeited your own freedom. Few people are able to do democratic work and fight unjust systems if they are firmly in debt to the very system they oppose. Live frugally and commit yourself to work that is dedicated to a just and fair world.

Study economics. It is not like reading racing forms or cowboy poetry, but in the short run just as valuable. However, often the best teachers are the critics and not the rah-rah men. The works of Noam Chomsky and Julianne Malveaux are a must. Mr. Chomsky and Ms. Malveaux are two of the few "true" public intellectuals who have a heart and live their politics. Other writers who also take on the uses and misuses of corporate, transnational and government power in a post-capitalist world are Adolph Reed, Cornell West, Michael Parenti, Paul Fussell, bell hooks, Molly Ivins and John Kenneth Galbraith. Finally, for the inside look at the inner workings of Wall Street, read Joseph Jett's *Black and White on Wall Street* written with Sabra Chartrond, and Julianne Malveaux's *Wall Street, Main Street and the Side Street: A Mad Economist Takes a Stroll.* For a thorough assessment of modern corporations study *When Corporation's Rule the World* by David C. Korten.

Remember, if we do not understand economics and

move quickly to check bad spending habits we will never truly be a liberated people. Our lives are controlled by politics as well as economics and it is not an accident that most of our political and cultural leadership are swimming in debt and deep ignorance. Most, if not all of this leadership has never met a payroll and are virtually dependent upon the same corporations, government and universities that they criticize. Yes, this a very complex subject and some of the strongest among us are in bed with each other and they are not missing a meal.

I end where I began. Life is short. The hard call is to say "no" to the inviting nonsense that crowd televisions, radios, billboards and computer screens, and "yes" to the wholeness of beauty, service, learning, love, productive work, and art.

# Laws of Empowerment

**One.**

*Always know more about your own culture than others. Critical thinking about one's self, people, culture and the world is imperative.* If you don't, those outside of your culture may try to use it against you. Cultural knowledge—yours and others, especially one's opponents—is critical in any kind of situation, whether a commercial battle for marketplace or a physical fight for dominance over individuals, armies or land. Study the cultures of the people closest to you. Fundamentally, the power of any people starts in the family. Empowered people have at least two families, the one they are born into and their "community" and/or cultural family. The most intelligent of African Americans are bi and tri-cultural. They know their own culture inside and out, and they know and have incorporated into their lives the culture of their oppressors and other free people in a wise manner.

Critical thinking is a learned activity. The serious study of the arts and humanities is the best place to start. As soon as possible the study of math, science, politics, world affairs and economics should be added. Deep contemplation on serious subjects is one of the ways to develop one's mind. The systematic reflection of one's self and our people's place in the world is an absolute prerequisite for liberation.

**Two.**

*Efficient actions are much more effective than loud words.* Yes, it is absolutely necessary that you are able to articulate your thoughts accurately and competently. However, if there is nothing but smoke behind your language, you will never succeed. Work hard and talk only when necessary. Outworking the talk in others will yield production and respect. Study, plan and grow in the execution of good ideas. Self-discipline is critical. Remember, the one freedom that is certain, non-discriminatory and touches all communities in the United States is the freedom to self-destruct. Avoid emotional poison that bad words, questionable associations and a drug dependent culture encourages.

### Three.

***Honesty is always the best policy.*** However, honesty must be practiced selectively and with care because people can use your truthfulness against you. The heart is always vulnerable in good people. Once your foes know your heart, they command a key "weakness" over your actions. The Taltec people of southern Mexico say, "Be impeccable with your words." It is a powerful concept. Your word is your bond. It is the way that you are ultimately defined. A person is remembered if he or she speaks the truth. A liar always walks in fear of his or her lies catching up with him or her. Do not speak bad words about yourself or others. If negative words are to be spoken against others, they must be the truth and spoken only to affect a greater good in you and others. If the truth had been spoken about Hitler, early and often, the Jewish Holocaust and the destruction of Europe may have been avoided. If the truth had been loudly spoken about the European trade in African men, women and children, maybe the middle passage, the transatlantic trade of African people, or that which has become known as the Maafa* could have been avoided.

---

*Great tragedy, unspeakable disaster, cataclysmic and extended nightmare.

**Four.**

***Be prepared in all situations.*** Never go into anything blind, whether it is a new job, a special date, interview for admittance to a top university, or physical combat. Be rigorous in preparation, bold in execution and
humble in winning. Try always to know as much about a
subject as possible and more than necessary. Most certainly, know more than your advisory. Always do your
best. Never be satisfied with being second, third or a former memory of what you or others used to be. Listen to
the elders of our culture and be in the forefront of the
men and women who honor them. Never settle for mediocrity in one's self, close friends or associates.

### Five.

***There is nothing virtuous about poverty.*** Most people in the world are poor, honorable and hard working. Their poverty for the most part is not of their making. Only fools openly and lavishly display wealth. The wealthiest people in the world are quite unknown to the average man and woman. They are generally only known by other people of wealth. Many Black people are known for wearing, driving, eating and playing hard with their money. Poor people wear their gold and the wealthy hide theirs. Wealth really means ownership. One must own one's self first. Then, understand and study the people who own and rule the world. They build and sell the houses, cars, gold, clothes, food and toys that we buy. They own land, real estate and the patriotic ideas that fuel the nation's cultural and commercial industry. They create the need for the sweet nothings and toys that clutter our homes. They control the compounded interests on our credit cards, bank loans and big ticket items we somehow cannot live without. Study the laws of wealth accumulation and build a life around not needing most of the money you earn.

Living in a world where most things and people are for sale means that one's options for empowerment are few. Recognize the traps of money, power and "butt selling politics." Learn to enjoy the finer jewels of life: nature, visual art, literature, film, good conversation, friendships, exercise, walking, travel, the beauty of other cultures and people. Value the expansion of your knowledge, the fundamental meaning of love, the wisdom of children and the sustaining and building aspects of faith. Remember, real wealth is knowledge and financial knowledge, if used wisely, leads to material wealth. However, beware of mercenaries, especially those that love, talk, work, and look like you.

**Six.**

*Nothing worthwhile is free.* If people are standing in line to give you something for nothing, it probably is not worth having. If people give you freedom, they can take it back. If the gift is material, spiritual, and worth your time, there is some cost involved. Yes, on occasion a family member or friend may give gifts of friendship and love—these are expected and reciprocated. But in the real world where antagonists, competitors, landlords, overlords, bosses, supervisors, loan sharks, educated capitalists, predators, co-workers, colleagues, team members, crooks, thieves, liars, disguised adversaries, and downright enemies exist and connive, you must be prepared to work hard and pay for all that is worthwhile. Dog-eat-dog competition is the way of much of the world. However, we must develop in our people the deep desire to take care of our own. From the very young to the elderly among us, we must look after each other in this competitive world. Always work toward ownership: ownership of self, space and community, businesses, institutions and ideas. Develop a consciousness in life of wealth creation and sharing.

**Seven.**

*Avoid predictability.* Always seek growth in your life. Understand the liberating and unlimited power of knowledge. Always be in a re-tooling mode, yet the master of several areas. It is said that we use less than twenty-five percent of our brain power. Men and women who are in powerful positions are able to move from position to position because they never stop learning and are not satisfied with mediocrity, in themselves and those close to them. They avoid "yes" people like they avoid quick diets. Each day, week, month and year, there must be measurable growth in you as a person and as a part of the profession(s) you have mastered. If one is to be predictable let it be in the arena of love, especially the love of family, one's people and all children.

### Eight.

***Work hard for a spiritual, physical and psychological balance and calmness in your life.*** Help those you love find the same. Study all of the known spiritual paths. Seek oneness with the best in people, always expecting the unexpected. Spiritual knowledge must never be used to imprison others or self. Share the good, knowing that evil in others and the world is only a layer away.

Stay in shape. Watch your weight. In the West, we need to consider eating less and restrict our diets to mainly fresh vegetables, fruits, whole grains, seeds, nuts, and legumes. Drink freshly made juices and at least a gallon of clean water a day. Try yoga and the martial arts to maintain weight, an inner oxygen flow, strength, confidence, and a delightful spirit. Incorporate meditation and deep prayer into your life. Look for friends who are like-minded. Goodness is everywhere, but evil is its shadow. Release your enlightenend spirit upon the world.

Be willing and in the forefront of sharing your money or wealth with the less fortunate by developing and/or supporting programs and institutions that speak directly to their needs and enlightenment. Work among the less fortunate in order to understand their needs, psychology and spirit. Work as much as possible with children, especially the children of the poor. Be prepared to invest your heart, mind and part of your resources to better their lives.

Study ethics, always be conscious of how your actions affect others. Be aware of the ever present temptations of money, sex, fame, status, and power. A moral life is a difficult life in a world ruled by greed, the pleasure principle and the ideas of small men and women. Remember, we live in a confused and manipulative world where healthcare for the world's majority is close to non-existent and mass public education needs help. In America, where the average child views over three thousand commercials a day and hundreds of homicides and fights via mass media, we do not need to look far for the reasons for confusion among them. It is indeed a wonder that our children can distinguish between the fine shades of acceptable behavior.

One of the fine shades of behavior is the ability to move in and out of many cultures and languages. We must be able to articulate our thoughts in the many colors of English. Black English is fine and legitimate at home and on the block. However, in order for a Black or Latino person to succeed in the United States, he or she must be able to distinguish himself or herself in the use of English. The only national or "right" form of spoken English is that of commerce or business. Yet, we all must understand and often be fluent in the language of law, academics, politics and health.

**Nine.**

*Control your anger.* Always check your negative emotions at the door. Public displays of anger or displeasure at the incorrect time speaks volumes about one's psychological well being. To be calm in the face of chaos puts you at a decided advantage in trying to understand and solve problems. To be objective in a burning building may allow you the seconds needed to find the best escape. Learn to smile naturally. A smile at the right time can brighten most situations and is the best way to show your human side. You'll be surprised at how good manners, politeness and a warm personality gives you a decided advantage in times of stress.

Racism and ethnic cleansing is universal. Be careful about using racism as the reason for all your problems. We cannot buy into victimology. If we see racism as the only factor stopping Black achievement, we by definition deny human complexity in all of its many permutations. The outward display of anger should always be tactical and strategic. One's personal problems or failures cannot be simply assigned to one's color, ethnic origin, religion, gender or age.

**Ten.**

***Understand leadership—its positives and its negatives.*** Leadership is not always knowing more than those you lead. It is convincing those with the best minds, the most creative ideas, the best work ethic and the material and financial resources to buy into your ideas. Learn how to read people. Be able to look into their eyes and hearts and listen to their minds and souls. Always move toward ownership and be willing to share ownership with those who deserve it. Black people make the music and others own it. Black people are the best athletes, but others own the teams and write the checks. Do good work. Be quick to praise and reward the people who work with, and for, you when they do good work. Be fair and just in assessing others.

Failure is only accepted if it is a lesson for greater awareness and success. The best of the best have failed often, but are quick learners. Their failures are far apart and have not crippled them emotionally or financially— hence they rise again. Boldness is absolutely necessary for good leadership and requires a high level of fearlessness, creativity and quick thinking.

Leadership in the African American community primarily comes from our religious community, the clergy. However, if people are to advance in a secular world ruled by CEOs, politicians, lawyers, military, academics, doctors, researchers, and the successful proponents of capitalism, they must have a leadership and a follow-ship schooled in the ways of this world. This is generally why a person with a quality Master of Business Administration degree is more respected in this culture than a person with a Master of Fine Arts from the same university. Capitalism rules the day in the West and fuels much of the arts, education, government, military and the underground economy.

Understand the psychology and needs of the poor, oppressed, dispossessed and enslaved. Seek the knowledge and information base of business owners, the wealthy and heads of corporations; not necessarily their value system, but understand the best of their winning ways. Understand the laws of accumulation. Few rich people succeed in this country (especially in the West) without help. The accumulative effect is really white peoples' affirmative action, which is built upon and advanced as a result of relationships that the founding patriarchs, grandpatriarchs, great-grandpatriarchs and great, great grandpatriarchs have developed over one thousand years of closed rulership of this nation and the Western world.

If you are among those producing and doing valuable work, you will have enemies. Be prepared to confront them and win; success is not an equal opportunity employer. Most successful people have had to fight hard and thus learned the art of warfare early. The prosperous continued to improve upon its lessons. This is partially why the ongoing development of one's intellect is so important. Be a student all of your life. A people will always be marginalized if their leaders are predictable, lazy, slow learners, non-thinkers, suckers for corrupting temptations, and most certainly if their leaders constantly misuse or abuse the power with which they have been entrusted. Leadership is always mindful of the other—family, friends or foe. Work to make your own luck. Life may indeed be a divine lottery. However, deep intellect, hard work and the ability to find a community of people who care about others and have ideas and resources to make constructive change for the majority (rather than the privileged few) is where you ultimately belong—if you care. A significant part of growing is to look critically at the people around you, to do an assessment and make the necessary personal decisions at the right time.

All in all, try to live a moral life based upon life-giving, life-saving and life-sustaining values and principles. Try to behave honorably and fairly in all of your life choices and actions. The hustlers run the world. You will be confronted with their truths, legislation, and con games every day. Stay focused and true to the highest values of a good and honorable people.

Smile, take a deep breath. Now, go to work. Study. Interact with your children. Bring something beautiful and beneficial into your life, neighborhood, community and world. Remember, winning is more meaningful if it contributes to all of us becoming better people.

# II.

## FINDING THE EXCEPTIONAL YOU

But there can be little doubt that figures like Baldwin and Malcolm X define the kind of work that has most influenced my own representations of the intellectual's consciousness. It is a spirit in opposition, rather than in accommodation, that grips me because the romance, the interest, the challenge of intellectual life is to be found in dissent against the status quo at a time when the struggle on behalf of underrepresented and disadvantaged groups seems so unfairly weighted against them.

—Edward W. Said
*Representations of the Intellectual*

# EDUCATION:
## Accepting No Excuses

Young brothers, I want to talk to you about one of life's most critical areas, education. If you don't know, you can't do. A person without knowledge will always be at the mercy of those with knowledge. How good you look, how well you are dressed, or the type of car you drive, matters little to those who rule. You can be the best dancer, the fastest runner, the basketball player with the quickest hands or the ladies' man with the best rap, winningest smile and most memorable kiss, but if you start young (letting your little head out think your big head) you are in for a short life of good times, many dead ends, and nothing jobs where you will work for people who care little about you or your pleasure seeking lifestyle.

In this life you can demand respect every hour of the day, each day of the year, and not move economically or socially from where you were born. Respect is earned and the road to a life where your family, friends and others will seek you out for advice, counsel, and use you and your life as an example for others is where you want to be. You cannot get there by mainly running the streets, basketball court, football or baseball fields. Wannabe pimps and good athletes are a penny a pound. Our communities and prisons are full of young men who at thirty-five are old in street knowledge and prison time and now are wondering what happened? Life, like time, waits on no one and the best way not to end up in the garbage cans of other people's systems is to plan and execute for yourself.

The main advantage of a quality education is the many options it provides. Yes, one can have a good education and still be a fool. However, the odds are against it. The key benefit of knowledge is that it frees you to think beyond the restriction of race, class, culture, religion and ethnic identity. I don't mean that it prepares you to run away. The right education provides possibilities and hope, introduces you to other people, other worlds and cultures and allows you to intelligently make decisions about your life that can place you among the builders and movers of the world rather than forever standing on corners talking bad about Black people, white people and wishing for this or that to materialize.

Consider the following in your search for a quality education:

· understand the absolute necessity of it

· understand what it takes and be willing to work harder than you ever worked

· be willing to endure ridicule and name-calling from friends and peers who have little vision or plans beyond the weekend

· find a community of learners to associate with, that is, seek out other young people on a leader ship track

· be willing to travel outside of your community to the best high schools, colleges and universities

· use the public and private libraries as well as the latest books and magazines wisely to help you in your quest to become the best

· learn to listen, learn to think critically

· continue to improve upon your reading and study habits—there are many books that can help you with this

· take the courses and find professors who will challenge you; to be the best you need instruction from the best—they don't have to be like you, or even like you, but only be willing to teach you

· find a wise and caring elder that you can trust and talk to—this may be a parent, grandparent, teacher, coach, librarian or policeman on the block

· fear being ignorant and the culture of ignorance

· understand that there are three types of intelligence—priviledge intelligence, intelligent intelligence and stupid intelligence—always use knowledge wisely in the best interest of yourself, family, community, people and nation. Develop the
habit of reading good books, newspapers and
magazines daily.

· learn to manage your time wisely, discipline in all
things is essential.

· don't take yourself too seriously—find friends that you
can relax with, enjoy life, remember you want to be a
healthy and whole person

· set goals and objectives; once met, set new ones

· learning is life long, once you have earned the degrees
or documents needed to pursue your profession, don't
stop growing; seek out professional organizations associated within your profession, and maintain a reading
schedule that includes literature outside of your spe-
cialty

None of this will be easy. As a six-foot, one-inch,
one hundred-forty pound, yellow-Black teenager, I knew
that the only way I was going to be accepted and respected by others in the Black movement of the sixties was to
prove to them and myself that I was worthy. I did this by

working hard, studying harder, dreaming big dreams, and acting on my dreams with ideas that led me to results. As the saying goes, "talk is cheap." Good acts require an investment of people, time, resources, work and commitment. Take a good long look at the Black world and ask yourself two questions. Why are we the butt of jokes for every ethnic group? What is it in the Black world that we produce, manufacture and distribute to be sold worldwide that benefits our people? Respect is earned and is determined by measurable production in all areas of human development. I hope you understand that a quality education is the first step on the road to the serious empowerment of yourself and our people. Remember, the one thing that can never be taken from you and will serve you for a lifetime is a quality education.

# I.Q. Starts At Home

Ever since I can remember, especially as a small child in the public schools of Detroit and Chicago, administrators, teachers and professional educators have questioned and doubted the intelligence of Black students. It does not seem to matter to many of them that their very doubt feeds into the children's concept of themselves and often plays out relatively early in how the children approach formal education. As today's headlines focus on the disparity between Black and white students on the A.C.T. and S.A.T. exams, professional educators across the nation meet to analyze the "problem." Many of them wonder secretly to themselves if Blacks can ever catch up. Having raised children of my own, worked in higher education for over thirty years, and co-founded two schools in Chicago (one private and the other charter), I come to this subject of test and test taking with some passion and a few reservations.

One of the fundamental problems with Black and poor students is that the vast majority of them have never been taught how to most effectively take exams. Most of these students do not come out of a test-taking culture. Many of them freeze and do poorly when confronted with the actual exam primarily because of a lack of test taking comfort. There are literally hundreds of books on the market that are published specifically to aid students in all of the national exams and many of the state mandated tests too. There are also courses taught throughout the year in most major cities to help prepare young people for this national rite of passage. All of this costs money and requires students and their parents to be aware of the examination industry that has grown up as a result of the importance placed on high test scores for acceptance into the best colleges and universities.

A great many African American, Latino and poor students go into these national and state exams cold. The results clearly document this. Many Black students do well in all of the critical categories of test taking, but as a group, Blacks fall short of their white and Asian classmates. Whenever these discussions arise, we must keep in mind that these scores are the average or median and do not represent the actual performance of millions of individual Black students who are intellectually sound and academically ready to rise and compete, and thus are the ones doing quite well in all disciplines at the nation's best colleges and universities.

What this discussion of test-taking and IQ really indicates is the absence of a culture of serious study. Most Black parents do demand that their children study beyond daily homework. Most parents do not create for their children an environment of quiet reflection—without television, CD player and random conversation. The huge struggles and commitments that most Black parents endured for material attainment is not often the same for intellectual attainment. We see across the country many Black middle-class communities with all of the outward trappings: well-kept homes with garages housing top-of-the-line cars and SUVs, the best furniture and computers, the best neighborhood churches and much more. Outwardly, this Black middle-class has materially made it. However, their neighborhood schools are often a mess and a national embarrassment.

That we have bought into material culture is not unusual. I am only suggesting that as we succeed in one area—the material—the universe of the intellect must not be minimized. Rather, the intellect must be given priority, especially in a world where one's color or race defines one. In generation's past, Black mothers and fathers (often with limited education themselves) repeatedly told Black children that they had to be twice as good as white children in school, scholarship, sports, character and work ethic. And yes, in today's world we still do have to be intellectually better.

Young brothers, our homes must become mini-learning institutions. We have to create in each home an environment that encourages and rewards us and our children for intellectual development just as we do for achievement in sports, entertainment and the arts.

We need a culture-of-study environment, which should include but not be limited to (before five years old), an introduction to the arts (music, dance, theater, film, poetry, fiction and creative non-fiction); regular out of neighborhood visits to museums, ethnic (e.g., Polish, Irish, Jewish, Italian, African and Caribbean) festivals; participation in citywide events, concerts, theater and dance groups; regular reading and learning in order to be comfortable with books, newspapers, magazines, quarterlies and computers; with routine visits to the local libraries to study. Early in our lives and in the lives of our children, libraries need to be understood as a place where they belong, a place where knowledge is available and inviting. Take advantage of youth and young adult programs at libraries, museums, churches, City Hall and park districts. Early involvement in the Boy Scouts and Girl Scouts, YMCA and YWCA, Boys and Girls Clubs and Rites-of-Passage rituals are all useful in the life skills instruction outside of the home. These activities will also aid in learning the geography of their cities—the lay of the land.

However, the most important tool for intellectual development is to be members of a family where adults are constantly seeking knowledge themselves, where parents and extended family equally seek a wholistic view of the world. Books, videos, CDs, magazines and newspapers along with the judicial use of the internet need to be natural in our homes. This must be coupled with engaging discussions of politics, history, psychology, art, civil service, math, foreign affairs and current events. A home where learning and knowledge accumulation is alive and well is what all children need. Mostly, your children need to be around family and friends who seek all kinds of knowledge, and who honor, love and respect young achievers.

You are only successful if you learn and use the

proven strategies and methods that work for millions of students across the world. Most people fear that which they know little about. There is a process to doing intellectual work. Test-taking could be like basketball. To become good, one has to dribble, shoot and study the techniques of the game. Test-taking is an intellectual game that requires years of preparation, deep study, practice, physical stamina and confidence. Remember, practice makes permanent.

Finally, the goal is not necessarily a high IQ score. The goal is to be prepared to function as intelligently as possible in doing one's life work. Each of us are unique products of our cultures and, likewise, we are all shaped by known and unknown factors in our environment. Yes, genes, biology and a loving home are critical. Yet, test-taking is a cultural and intellectual act that should not be minimized. Academic tracking in school starts early in this culture, and as parents you need to be aware of how your children are being positioned as a result of their test results.

There is a saying that you are what you eat. To expand upon that truism, your children are also what they read, think about, study, listen to, play with, watch, taste, love, feel and see. And, all of these start at home.

# Reading

It is highly unlikely that you can achieve the goals that your parents or care-givers set for you if you can't read well. If you do not study the words of great and not so great writers, poets, scholars, critics, teachers and journalists, I doubt if you will fully be able to master the nuances of this culture, or any culture, and reach your full potential.

Contrary to misinformed and street belief, reading is not an alien activity. Reading is not only for rich and middle-class white people or Black people trying to be white. To be able to read and intelligently articulate your thoughts puts you in the top twenty percent of the world's population; most of the world's people cannot read or write at an eighth grade level.

The quest for knowledge starts at birth. From babies' natural urges for food, water, love and human connection and human conversation to their innate need to define themselves and their surroundings. All play important roles in the preparation for reading. Parents who talk to and read to their children early are positioning their children in a universe where words, language, text and writing rule. Parents who take the time to answer and encourage their children's questions undoubtedly understand the critical desire growing minds have for new information. Between birth and the age of six years, the individual's brain is thirsting for knowledge and either continues, slows or completely shuts down depending on how it is fed in the early years. This is not a mystery.

The acquisition of knowledge starts, manifests and endures through the play with words—oral and written. One's introduction to the sun, earth and its sounds, stars, waterfalls, forests, animals, insects and all that goes into making this a beautiful or ugly world is intricately involved in whether a child will master the art and science of reading early or later in life. Early readers who are surrounded with early love, security, informed instruction and delicate encouragement do have a head start. Reading is truly a learned activity and there is a fragile line between those who end up reading well and loving to read, and those who barely get by or end up hating reading because no one took the time to properly teach them.

Whether you are examining the intricate text of the *Bible, Torah or Koran*, deciphering the *I Ching* or *Bhagavad-Gita* or discovering your connectedness to the literature of our best writers, poets, playwrights, journalists and scholars, your ability to deeply absorb the language(s) of a text depends greatly on your reading aptitude—which grows as you read, think and discuss the texts. Obviously, your schooling is fundamental to how you approach reading. If your first teachers are excited about the possibility of expanding your mind through the introduction of language and literature, better are the chances that you will later find your way among books, journals, magazines, newspapers, etc.

When I think of the magic and endurance of the literature of Gwendolyn Brooks, Claude McKay, John O. Killens, Margaret Walker and Melvin B. Tolson, I am reminded of their magical use of language, their unique ability to turn words into motivating signposts that encouraged others to excel. When reading Zora Neale Hurston, Robert Hayden, Malcolm X and John Henrik Clarke I think of the ultimate force of their learned minds, the quality of their arguments and their ability to give us new insights into the issues of their times. Richard Wright, Chester Himes, Frank Yerby, Shirley Ann Williams, Margaret Danner and Toni Cade Bambara are not with us anymore, but their stories and poems are. Their love and respect for Black people glows in their language about us, to us.

I still look forward to the unique adventure in ideas while reading writers who were my contemporaries: Leon Forrest, Etheridge Knight, Larry Neal, Audre Lorde, Addison Gayle Jr., Hoyt W. Fuller, James Baldwin, Dudley Randall, Ann Petry and Dorothy West. We ate the same food, endured the same racism, laughed at some of the same jokes. Yet, they found a way in their language to leave us their memories, their short and long tales, their secrets. The writer and poet Reynolds Price, commenting on the loss of imagination among young people, feels that the major cure for ignorance and the almost total addiction to television and its commercials is good reading. He writes in *Feasting the Heart*,

Short of destroying all television sets, computer screens, and video games, I'd suggest at least one countervailling therapy: good reading, vast quantities of active or passive reading—and reading which is, in part, guided by a child's caretakers. No other available resource has such a record of benign influence on maturation. Give every child you cherish good books—human stories—at every conceivable opportunity. If they fail to read them, offer bribes—or whatever other legal means—to help them grow their own imaginations in the slow solitude and silence that makes for general sanity.

If I had to name one life skill that is absolutely critical to your search for wholeness and empowerment in today's world it would be reading. Young men, elevate your reading to the level you play basketball and chase sisters. Be as serious about reading as you are about learning to drive or buying clothes. I can promise this: if you learn to read well, and in doing so learn to love and respect literature, you will be surprised at the result. Your self-confidence will skyrocket with each writer, poet, playwright, scholar and journalist whose work you consume.

Remember, reading good literature is like a million answers to the questions you always wanted to ask but were afraid to, for fear of sounding ignorant or stupid. The acquisition of knowledge via reading is like preventive medicine for the mind, spirit and body. Read like you eat. In fact, read more; eat less. The nourishment offered by good books only puts weight on a hungry mind.

At the end of this book is a Selected Bibliography and Suggested Reading list. Below are newspapers, magazines, journals and some electronic media that you need to be aware of if you are to be as fully informed as possible.

### Newspapers

*New York Times* (the nation's paper of record. The coverge of African Americans is not a balanced one or one that is truly national). However, Bob Herbert, Margo Jefferson, Anthony Lewis and Brent Staples all do their best to represent a Progressive point of view.

*Wall Street Journal* (primarily concerned with the nation's economic state and is considered by many as the first word on the state of modern capitalism).

*Chicago Tribune* (covers the nation and has strong international reports but major focus is Chicago and the midwest). Clarence Page is must reading.

*Los Angeles Times* (also has a national and international coverage but strongest area is Los Angeles, California and the west coast).

*Chicago Daily Defender* (the only daily Black newspaper in the country. The great journalist Vernon Jarrett appears weekly)

*Amsterdam News* (New York City)

*Michigan Chronicle* (Detroit, Michigan)

In fact, all Black newspapers in America need to be read and supported.

## Magazines

*The Nation*—Patricia J. Williams is must reading

*The Progressive*—carries the works of Adolph Reed and June Jordan

*In These Times*—the fine journalist Salim Muwakkil is a senior editor

*Mother Jones* (left of center politically)

*Black Enterprise*

*The Black Scholar*—the primary quarterly of Black ideas

*Black Issues in Higher Education*—the leading magazine in Black education (published twice monthly)

*Black Issues Book Review*—the leading magazine in Black books, literature, and publishing

*Quarterly Black Books Review*—an important magazine on Black books and ideas

*Ebony* —the oldest and leading Black monthly, the great historian Lerone Bennett Jr. is its editor.

*Jet*—the only Black news weekly

*Essence*—the leading Black woman's monthly

*The Black Collegian*—all Black students need to be aware of this important magazine

*Extra!*—a very serious critique of media

*Z magazine* (left of center politically)

*The Weekly Standard* (right of center politically)

*The National Review* (right of center politically)

*The Gaither Reporter*—an important independent journal

*Crisis magazine*—the voice of the NAACP and Black community for close to one hundred years

*Commentary*—Jewish, right of center politically)

*The Atlantic Monthly*

*Harper's*

*Tikkun* (Jewish, left of center politically and highly spiritual)

*Utne Reader*

*The New Republic*

*Sojourner*—a magazine of faith, culture and politics

*The American Prospect*

*The New Yorker*—the leading cultural weekly of extremely creative fiction, non-fiction, poetry and cartoons)

*The Sun*—independent journal of ideas

*Columbia Journalism Review* (media review)

## Journals

*African American Review* (Indiana State University, excellent for scholars)

*American Legacy*

*Warpland: A Journal of Black Literature and Ideas* (Chicago State University)

*Souls: A Critical Journal of Black Politics, Culture and Society* (Columbia University)

*Poetry* (major journal of American poetry out of Chicago)

*Brilliant Corners: A Journal of Jazz and Literature*

*WQ: The Wilson Quarterly, Surveying the World of Ideas*

*The Paris Review*

*The Ohio Review*

*Tin House*

*The Iowa Review*

*Pan American: Journal for Writers and Readers*

*Poets and Writers: What Creative Writers Need to Know*

*Glimmer Train*

*Triquarterly*

*Granta*

*Obsidian* (North Carolina State University)

*Mosaic Literary Magazine*

*Callaloo (a major journal of African American literature)*

*Rosebud: The Magazine for People who Enjoy Good Writing*

*The Western Journal of Black Studies* (Washington State University)

*Transition: An International Review*

*The New York Review of Books*

*Yes*—a journal of positive futures

Be very discriminating about your reading. There are literally thousands of newspapers, magazines, journals and other reading materials available at any good library. I also strongly suggest that you consider listening to and/or looking at:

Black talk radio in your area
National Public Radio (NPR-generally on FM around
      91.5—*Morning Edition, All Things Considered,*
*Fresh Air* and *Talk of the Nation* are fair-minded and
inclusive)
Public Television (PBS)
C-Span
C-Span II and III (Book weekend on C-Span II is a must
for serious readers.)

The internet has the opportunity to become the most
democratic of all media, but one must be critical in the
use of this important media.

# WRITING

The second millennium that we have entered is only on the Western calendar. Civilizations of Asia, Africa and South America have experienced many millenniums. The problem facing us is that the great majority of the people in the United States have little, if any, knowledge of cultures and people outside of the West. Most of us are in the West and the West is in us, and few of us have had the privilege and benefit of experiencing other people, languages and cultures. And, the sad fact is that most of us are satisfied. We spend a small fortune (by world standards) on the material fixtures of our class rather than traveling and educating ourselves about the people of Asia, Europe, Africa, South America and elsewhere.

Writers by definition are curious people. The best of them are like sponges and absorb whatever enters their space of activity. Some writers view their avocation, craft or art as a tool to educate others; academic, nature, travel, technical and sacred writers fall into this category. Creative writers are about inventing known and unknown worlds for the readers' entertainment, enjoyment and enlightenment. The more serious of them also write to feed the readers' mind with unfamiliar worlds of historical fiction and speculative fiction. They infuse their novels and short stories with ideas carefully wrapped in competent and inviting prose. The best literary non-fiction writers tackle most subjects with the heart, eye, ear, mind, emotions and techniques of fiction writers. They seek to make their subjects come alive, yet do not stray too far from documented facts. Poets, the lesser read of creative writers, use language in a minimalist manner. They record the world as they witness it, retell it in highly compressed metaphors and language that requires a commitment to reading that most people are not prepared for. Thus, most people have little appreciation for the beauty and mystery of poetry. The best poets understand this distance between reader and poetry and adjust accordingly.

The writers' stories are many. They write of the movement of storms and the stillness of the wind. Some examine subjects as far apart as spiritual geology and the changing of diapers. Others capture the intimate feelings of mad people and the magic of saints that work and walk among us. The best of our writers weave mythic layers that challenge us to be better, more informed than we think possible. Like good music, the quality of a writer's craft varies depending largely upon his or her training and preparation, knowledge base, seriousness and the largeness of one's ideas, as well as the ingredients that move one's heart, and soul. Like hot whole grain bread for the body, we receive from our best writers' heated stories and poems ready to nourish the mind and spirit.

Some writers bring us marvelous stories and poems that enlighten and ground us in the culture that we are born into. Others travel the world seeking to find the beauty and mystery in other people so as to enlarge themselves as well as their readers. In the West we are blessed with thousands of publishing outlets: magazines, newspapers, journals, books, newsletters, world wide web and much more. Deciphering quality from the junk is part of the reading process. For example, in 2001 over 65,000 books in just about every conceivable subject were published by corporate, independent and small publishers. Couple this with thousands of daily and weekly newspapers and magazines, with hundreds of monthly and quarterly journals that flood most good newsstands and bookstores. Add to this the explosion of writers on the world wide web and the critical question is, "what does one read?"

My point is that most knowledge is created, communicated, stored, classified and disseminated by way of the written word. Writing is hard, sometimes boring and highly intricate work. We tend to appreciate teachers, surgeons, CEOs and architects, but writers receive little acknowledgement and less compensation for their work. However, teachers, surgeons, architects and yes, even CEOs could not excel without books.

As we experience the Western millennium—one that gave us printing presses, computers, distant learning, paperback books, Amazon.com and mass education—let us not forget the fiction writers, scholars, poets, dramatists, screen writers, journalists and others who toil daily in the unsung melodies of their minds hoping to be read by this generation of decision makers and creators making ready for millennium three thousand.

It seems to me that the larger question at all times in the psyche of the best poets, writers, critics, artists, scholars, and teachers is, "how do we arrive at the truth?" In finding the truth, how do we translate truth so that it empowers people to do good work, so as to positively impact on public and private policies and structures that influence and direct their lives?

This issue of finding common truth is a difficult one. We, those thinkers and writers endowed and blessed with the talents, skills, cultural insights and urgencies, resources, and time to engage in this important pursuit, approach it in our own individual ways. Each of our disciplines may seek the same end: truth. However, our understanding of it in a multicultural world is often intellectually and pragmatically at odds. Because of their cultural orientation, education, and commitment, good people with a common aim often arrive at the same corner in the same city with different expectations, concerns, and conclusions, but all with questions and a willingness to listen and dialogue.

There is this grand tradition in this country of a "free" and informed press. *This is no small right.* The ability of a great many people to argue, debate, write, publish, and thus capture the essence of our best minds in print, allowing the reading public the time to study the core of their thinking, represents the cornerstone of a democratic society.

The reality for me, after thirty-nine years of direct political and cultural struggle and travel that has taken me to Africa, Asia, Europe, South and Central America and just about every state in the United States and Canada, all showered in deep study and conversation with some of the best minds of any century that real democracy requires and demands nothing less than the truth. The best of our writers give us their souls with each book, play, short story, poem or article that delves deeply into the mystery of the human spirit. If a person carefully reads Gwendolyn Brooks, Toni Morrison, John A. Williams, John O. Killens, Michael Parenti, Carter G. Woodson, Amiri Baraka, Noam Chomsky, Edward Said, bell hooks, August Wilson, Richard Wright, Margaret Walker, Maulana Karenga, Arundhati Roy, Alice Walker, Ishmael Reed, Derrick Bell, W.E.B. DuBois and countless others, I challenge him or her to speak nonsense or to spend hour after hour, lifeless in front of television or video games. Good writing fuels the mind, challenges falsehoods and questions authority; anything less is an insult to the human spirit and its capacity for intellectual empowerment and social change that benefits the great majority, rather than line the pockets of the corrupt and greedy few.

Writers who matter and endure, reject righteous sainthood and any elevation to a status that removes them from their people, their readers and a world that fuels their imagination. Writing, like music is a calling to its practitioners. They wear their art like hand made shoes and are identified with it like J.J. Johnson to trombone, Melvin B. Tolson to poetry and Katherine Dunham to dance. Real writers breathe and exhale words and ideas; to be published and read is the closest we can get to a serious, yet different, love affair that our mates and the reading public will accept. We write to live and live to write. The mystery of this art is so complex that few of us ever acquire a readership or make a living from it, but like sand on a beach, we never go away and we are universal.

# Free Public Libraries:
## Democracy's Real Test

My voracious reading habit and the lack of friends as a child accompanied me into adulthood. Coming up, I was always a stranger in my own home. I developed quite early the practice of reading any and everything in a cultural environment where reading was not encouraged or rewarded by family, friends or teachers. I read newspapers, dream books, racing forms, magazines, the Bible, books forced on us in elementary school and those books denied me by adults because of my age. When I discovered the Detroit Children's Library and Detroit's Main Public Library at the age of twelve, it was like hitting the numbers (today's lottery). There, I was the perpetual winner.

Unlike most of the young white students that visited the Detroit Public Library in the 1950s, I was not able to attach myself to a librarian who would help guide my reading. There were not any Black librarians on or near the main desk with whom I could connect. Often, the white librarians, mostly women—viewed my constant visits as a dilemma. This was during the time of America's apartheid. My presence was barely tolerated and generally ignored.

My mother was very much dysfunctional by this time. Her drinking and drug-addiction had taken over her life. Most of her days and nights were devoted to looking for the next high. My father was an absent entity who surfaced in extreme emergencies—and then just to drop a few coins peppered with lots of criticism. The Detroit Public Library became a home away from home, a place where I could briefly leave the harsh realities of my days and nights.

Like most poor people we moved almost yearly, relocating in the same general area because of the restricted living space for Black folks. As a young boy, I viewed this as luck. It kept me in the same schools, and I stayed in walking distance of the main library. The library became my intellectual refuge and a point of cultural departure and stability in my young life.

I outgrew the children's library rather quickly and began frequenting the adult library while in elementary school. Before I started junior high, I knew the ins and outs of the main library like the back streets of Detroit I maneuvered to get there. A young boy without street attachment (gangs or youth groups) meant that I had to be very careful about where I walked. I learned quickly. My routes became second nature. Almost intuitively, I knew the best time of day it was safe to walk in certain areas. I developed all kinds of shortcuts and detours that allowed me to be as anonymous as possible. A young boy with an arm full of books was always ripe for ridicule, attack or recruitment by local gangs.

I was somewhat known in the area because my mother was a popular barmaid at one of the notorious nightspots. It was my mother who encouraged me to read. Even in the deepest part of her sickness she understood that I needed much more than the public schools could provide. Also, my sister, a year and a half younger than I, was one of the "finest" girls in the city. Because of her I experienced a rather dubious distinction. First, most of the older boys wanted to meet her and would approach me for an introduction. Second, when she didn't want to be bothered, she would use me to threaten them. "If you don't leave me alone, I'll tell my brother," she'd say.

Often I had to fight and run my way to and from school. This forced me to carry all kinds of weapons: kitchen knives, broken door locks that I would use like brass knuckles. I was attacked often. At six-feet one-inch and weighing one hundred forty pounds, I, a light-skinned "Negro," did not strike fear into the hearts of my peers. I was forced to learn rather quickly how to talk or "signify" my way out of most street situations. This use of language as a means of protection started early in my life, and my familiarity with language and literature, specifically Black literature, helped tremendously.

A good many of the local gang members were poor students and required help with exams and papers, and I would either sell my services or offer them free, depending on the circumstances. This helped me only among the "brothers" who were still in school. By the time they reached high-school age, most of the gang members had decided that street employment was more lucrative in the short run than sitting in dull classrooms six hours a day listening to teachers who felt imprisoned themselves. The Detroit (and later Chicago) Public Library aided me to no end in supplementing my education. The card catalog was my early world wide web. I had at my finger tips the key to where all the books were.

Most of my homework was completed in the public library. Acquiring an "A" average in junior high was not difficult in this environment. It was also rather deceptive in measuring my own intelligence because the I.Q. bar had been lowered far below the best schools in the system. Obviously, I was not aware of this at the time and only began to understand my un-preparedness when I was admitted to one of the best high schools in the state of Michigan, Cass Tech.

Cass Tech in the late 1950s was a magnet school that attracted the best students from the neighborhood schools. Students had to have a minimum of a "B" average to take the admission exam. Cass was unusual in that it was both a technical school and primarily a college prep institution. Each student majored in a particular field. Since I was a halfway decent trumpet player in junior high (and since I was without any counseling) I chose music as my major.

My frequent visits to the Detroit Public Library helped me to endure my year at Cass Tech, a highly racist school that taught me that I was not wanted and that I needed to understand this system in order to be competitive. I lived in an environment where I made all the important decisions about my life. No one else in my

family was in a position to advise me. I left Cass Tech
after my freshman year for a neighborhood high school
because I didn't have a support system and my situation
at home had gotten considerably worse. My mother's
drug habit had completely taken over her life. My sister,
now fourteen was pregnant by one of the major gang
leaders in Detroit. This was a catastrophe. During those
days, it was considered taboo for girls to have children
outside of a traditional marriage.

As the "man" of the house, I went looking for the
father to uphold the "honor" of our home. I found him
and confronted him with her pregnancy, which he didn't
deny. I commenced to try and break his jaw, a move not
in my best interest, but consistent with the code of the
streets. Even if I was not physically equipped to enforce
it, I had to do what was expected of the "men" at that
time. I endured one of the worst beatings a boy of six-
teen could tolerate from a twenty-year-old man. Upon
returning home and explaining my bruised and disfig-
ured face to my slightly inebriated mother, I received
another whipping for getting whipped.

I left home that Saturday afternoon and went to the
only place in my young life that I knew would not be critical of me or my actions, the Detroit Public Library. I
remember locating Mark Twain's *Adventures of
Huckleberry Finn* on the shelves and finding a quiet
space to read. I lost myself in the fiction of a white progressive writer who tried to paint some Blacks and
whites as victims of a culture and nation that they had no

control over. After three hours of reading with a few naps in between, I left the library feeling that my life had changed considerably. In a fast-changing world, I had a few more choices to control my destiny than "Nigger Jim"; literature had taught me that, and the two whippings I experienced that day confirmed in my young mind the realities of my life.

The year was 1958 and I had accepted, even within the critical climate of racism, that free public libraries would be in my life forever. As I walked home that Saturday evening with two books under my arms, it hit me that all I needed to acquire vast quantities of knowledge about the world was a library card—which was free. On that day, even the white librarians had softened their responses to me. As I checked out the books, quiet and unassuming but clearly wounded physically and psychologically, their smiles denoted for the first time in four years, welcome.

During the walk home, my short life passed in front of me. I now accepted the hard fact that I was on my own and the only thing that would protect me was a superior knowledge base. This knowledge would allow me personal and professional options other than the streets. For a poor Black boy, the free public library was my equalizer and the best example of real democracy at work for poor people who lacked the resources to buy all the books they needed or desired.

During these early years, I started collecting books. Most of the clothes I wore were bought at second hand

Salvation Army stores. At all of the Salvation Army stores, there were book sections where hundreds of books and magazines were available at a fraction of the list price. I remember finding first editions of work by Frank Yerby, Richard Wright, W.E.B. DuBois and others for fifteen to twenty-five cents each. For ten cents, I acquired a used copy of *Rising Above Color* edited by Philip Henry Lotz; the importance of this collection is that the editor had essays by George Washington Carver, Marian Anderson, W.E.B. DuBois, Samuel Coleridge-Taylor, Richard Allen, Frederick Douglass, Paul Laurence Dunbar, James Weldon Johnson and others. This was an early introduction to the original thinking and to the complexity of some of our most talented people. Before the 1950s ended, I had quite a collection numbering about one hundred and ten books. To this day, second hand bookstores remain one of my favorite places to visit and collect my thoughts, as well as good books.

In 1959 my mother was dead, my sister's son was close to a year old, and her son's father had abandoned his responsibility to pursue other women and the street life of Detroit, Michigan. I left Detroit via the Greyhound bus for Chicago (where my father lived) to begin a new life. I quickly found the Hall Branch Library at 48th and Michigan Avenue which had one of the most comprehensive collections of Black literature, history and culture. I was in my last year of high school and finished a two-year program at Chicago's Dunbar Vocational High School in one year and a summer partially because of my intellectual center, aquired by outside reading. The Hall Branch Library had two Black librarians who helped me. Vivian Harsh, the head librarian was receptive and helpful. However, it was Charlemae H. Rollins who helped to guide my reading and encouraged me to write my "little poems." I had grown into an assiduous reader. "Never to leave home without a book" was my mantra. A habit that has served me well. Today, reading is just as important as eating and sleeping.

The free library system of America, along with public schools remain the cornerstones and hope for poor and middle class people, newly arrived immigrants and all citizens who value freedom. In the final countdown, the availability of life-giving, life-saving and life affirming knowledge levels the playing field for millions of folks systematically locked out of this system. For me libraries—and the information they contain and freely share—represent the real liberated zones of this nation. When public education is compromised and the budget and staff hours of public libraries are severely reduced, we are, indeed, in trouble. Bond with your children by visiting libraries regularly. Proudly, with them, use your library cards and with them especially with the very young do the one thing that guarantees to elevate and free their minds, read, read and read. Whatever your next move is, your local library may help you on the journey.

# Intellectuals I

There is an unspoken but loud environment of anti-intellectualism in many segments of the Black community. A young man's ability to dunk basketballs, hit home runs, score touchdowns or run a hundred yards in record time is seen in some quarters as far too significant achievements. On the other hand, for example, when young Black men visit me at home, Third World Press or Chicago State University and take notice of shelves of books, their first question is "have you read them all?" However, they never ask "why?"

The accumulation of knowledge for its own sake is not totally alien to the Black community. Yet, it takes a back seat to most people's interest in learning a profession or craft to acquire employment, status, economic stability and comfort. This is understandable in a commercial and consumer-driven culture. But as a result of this state of affairs, Black intellectuals have little power or influence on national, political, or economic policies.

Few think tanks exist in our communities. Most Black colleges and universities are cut in the same mold as their white counterparts, minus the resources and nurturing of their intellectuals and philosophers. In fact, only a few Black universities actually have departments of philosophy. Most of the nationally known and respected Black philosophers work at predominately white universities or independent white think tanks. This search for knowledge for its own sake and the drive to answer difficult questions is viewed by many uninformed African Americans as acting white and thus dismissed as insignificant. Yet, without much thought, most of the marginally educated recognize the names Socrates, Plato, Aristotle, Spinoza, Locke, Kant, Hegel, Adams, Machiavelli, Russell, James, Dewey, Emerson, Thoreau, Jefferson, Nietzsche, Schopenhauer, Herodotus and Santayana as philosophers and thinkers of European and European American persuasion. Because of the enormous impact these men have had on Western thought and culture, you cannot matriculate through the doors of any competent high school, college or university in the West without closely examining at least some of their ideas.

The study of their ideas in a highly racist context helped to create millions of Black people without knowledge of themselves, thereby educating most of us into a culture where we felt inferior and always rejected. For me, a poet and full-time thinker about the lives of Black people, I found myself as a young man decidedly disadvantaged until I accidentally came across the voluminous works of W.E.B. DuBois and the revolutionizing ideas of Frantz Fanon. Both these men were highly educated in the European tradition, but they somehow managed to devote their lives to the scholarly inquiry, activism, and writing about the conditions, lives and souls of Black folks. In studying the works of DuBois and Fanon, both internationalist and Africanist, I learned that poor people did not need to be confined to the definitions, mythologies and stereotypes of outsiders who cared little about us. The lack of respect for Black people and our contributions to world civilization by the ruling elite and their supporters is criminal, anti-scholarly, racist and small-minded. However, DuBois and Fanon exhibited in their intellectual work and activity a certain boldness, independence and freedom of thought. The range of their thinking went far beyond what our oppressors expected of Blacks of the time. DuBois and Fanon went for big answers and played on both a local, national and international intellectual field.

The large questions of life, death. and countless concerns rip at the nerve endings of an emerging twenty-first century world: the existence of a God or Gods; the understanding of color and race ideology; the workings of and the contributions of a democratic and civil society; the importance of culture in the moral and ethical fabric of a people; the necessity and requirements of education; the unique responsibility of Black women and men locked in a white supremacist culture; the meaning of being an African in a European world; the function of money and wealth in the political life; the requirements of accurate history and psychology for wholeness and health; the reasons for rampant anti-intellectualism in the modern Black community; comprehending the necessity of doubt and skepticism in a secular and consumer society; understanding the rush by many to believe rather than think and question; the importance of manhood, womanhood, family, parenting, spiritual and service institutions; the importance of maintaining a working and fair government; and the ethical questions emanating from biology and gene research. These questions are not new. However, they must continuously be revisited from one political and cultural context to the next.

The need for indigenous and complementary values in a multi-cultured, multi-racial and multi-religious world requires that people read more than newspapers, Bibles, Korans, Torahs, magazines, and comic books (or sit transfixed at every professional ball game or soap opera that is televised). The requirements of freedom, in all its multi-layered definitions in a complex and diverse society should be of interest to all. Freedom requires liberated thinkers. Liberated thinkers are needed to understand why many non-white people unknowingly contribute to and participate in their own destruction. Gender awareness and its lack of discussion in the Black world must be a concern of our greatest thinkers. Concepts of honor, betrayal, trust, integrity, honesty, competition and commitment require that people study, discuss, debate and organize together. Individuals hitting the most web sights in a twenty-four hour day is clearly not enough. Organized and unorganized contemplation by Blacks, individually and in groups, on the state of the world is critical. Only through liberating ideas are we motivated to act in our own and others' liberation.

Over the last century or so there has been an explosion of original thinking, writing and the dissemination of radical and new ideas in the Black world by men and women of deep color. In the last fifty years alone, we have produced literally tens of thousands of historians, political scientists, philosophers, sociologists and scientists in all disciplines, as well as artists, poets, novelists, actors, musicians, dancers, engineers and architects. We now have a solid working community of African, African American and African Caribbean philosophers; men and women who love wisdom, who accumulate knowledge for knowledge's sake and use their minds to do research that address and answer many of the above concerns. Just as importantly, they asked their own questions and have given rigorous thought to finding answers and solutions.

As a result, there is now name-recognition of some of our great thinkers: Martin Delaney, Frederick Douglass, Alexander Crumwell, Edward Wilmont Blyden, David Walker, Carter G. Woodson, W.E.B. DuBois, Frances Ellen Watkins, Alain Locke, Anna Julian Cooper, J.A. Rodgers, Mary Church Terrell, Ida Wells-Barnett, Melvin B. Tolson, Rayford Logan, E. Franklin Frazier, Martin Luther King, Jr., Frantz Fanon, Malcolm X, Paulie Murray, Louis Armstrong, James Baldwin, Cheikh Anta Diop, John Henrik Clarke, John Oliver Killens, Chancellor Williams, Langston Hughes, Gwendolyn Brooks, John Coltrane, and Amos N. Wilson, to name a few who are now honored ancestors.

Those philosophers and thinkers who are still with us and are productive, number in the thousands. Their works have helped to open door after door in all areas of human endeavor. Some of them are Adrian M.S. Piper, Angela Davis, Michele Wallace, Maulana Karenga, Wade Nobles, Andrew Billingsley, Asa G. Hilliard III, John Edgar Wideman, August Wilson, Marimba Ani, Jacob H. Carruthers, Ayi Kwei Armah, Wole Soyinka, Delores Aldridge, John Hope Franklin, Cornel West, Ellis Cose, Keith Gilyard, Paula Giddings, Beverly Guy-Sheftall, bell hooks, Fred Hord, Lerone Bennett Jr., Harold Cruse, Nell Irvin Painter, Barbara A. Sizemore, Ron Daniels, Leonard Harris, Carole D. Lee, Ngugi Wa Thiong'o, Walter Mosley, Geneva Smitherman, William R. Jones, Barbara Smith, Darlene Clark Hine, Carl C. Bell, Ronald Walters, Alice Walker, Amiri Baraka, Toni Morrison, Randall Robinson, Molefi Asante, Raymond A. Winbush, Frank M. Reid III, Clarence James, Naim' Akbar, June Jordan, James Turner, Joe McMilliam, George Yancy, Joy James, Jeremiah A. Wright Jr., Useni Eugene Perkins, Yosef Ben Jochannon, Lewis R. Gordon, Vilbert L. White Jr., and Joyce Mitchell Cook, to name a very few.

Their love of learning, their search for truth and active participation in intellectual and cultural struggles have been our major weapons in the fight against oppression and evil. Most of the men and women listed here have spent their lives in their chosen discipline earning formal and informal Ph.Ds with continued post doctoral work. However, a great many others remain talented and committed "outsiders" who as in all cultures are the real visionaries that produce new ideas and push the "insiders" to their limits. Most of them are tangential to the circle, keeping it smooth while working overtime to enlarge its circumference. They understand the need to include people who think and believe that there is room for all who are seeking sunshine, love, beauty, fairness and enlightened empowerment in their lives. This is not insignificant work. Rather, it is mind-driving, direct action that transcends the pitfalls of ego, greed, selfishness and all isms which tribalize people into enclosed caves.

These women and men do not seek outlandish rewards, but simply love wisdom, liberation and independence. Their love of knowledge is fundamental to their search for truth. The liberating ideas of "their truths" propel serious men and women to take ownership of their lives and to stand boldly and responsibly for those less fortunate persons caught in the many traps of a commercial culture. You can do no less.

# INTELLECTUALS II

The major role of intellectuals, especially the powerful, is to find the truth and speak the truth to all, as plainly, forcefully, directly and honestly as possible. It is the unique responsibility of intellectuals to be an example of the truth that they know, respect and speak. This is not easy because all truths are not transferable from culture to culture, or between men and women, or neighborhoods in the same city or nation.

However, there are some common truths or beliefs that are shared and ones that most people and cultures agree upon, ponder and question. Some of them are: the role of God(s) and faith, life and death, good and evil, beauty and ugliness, questions of honesty, integrity, and kindness. The innocence of children and the need for quality education are shared concerns. The necessity of love, caring and security, the need for fruitful work and a work ethic are universal. Family and friendship, respect for individual rights and law, respect for personal property and public space are debated internationally. Respect for life, freedom and democracy; honoring parents, adult nurturers, care givers and elders are now on most thinking people's minds. Respect for gender strengths and differences, respect for teachers, respect for healers—spiritual, medical and mental; respect for lifelong learning and knowledge acquisition are not only concerns of the West. The necessity of money and economics, the role of sports and play are reported on daily in most countries. The importance of minority thought and populations, the meaning of land, agriculture and national identity remain hot subjects in most universities. Reflections on war, violence, resolution and peace, the place of commerce and greed continue to demand quality debate. Questions of that which is good, just and correct for a diverse population, and the indispensable connection of culture to people are concerns that keep thinking people working. These are just a minute number of questions that serious intellectuals think, write and debate about hourly of each day.

Thinking people come from all walks of life. It doesn't matter what a person's color, religion, politics, economic status, gender, nationality, weight or diet is, serious thinkers are everywhere. However, there are professional and public intellectuals who are paid quite well to teach, do research, write and publish books and articles, attend conferences, argue before Congress and other private and closed bodies, frequent the Sunday mornings' and weekly evening television and radio talk shows and act as if they have an answer for all questions. The op-ed pages of the major newspapers publish their observations and solutions to current problems. However, most working intellectuals in the academy, national and local think tanks, in government as well as independent researchers see their work as part of their life's mission and most would do it with or without great remuneration. They are often unknown outside of their fields, yet many are honored and are responsible for serious intellectual development in all areas of life.

Intellectuals, out of necessity and quite natural to their work, are often very private and independent people. Intellectuals are fundamental to a growing and diverse society. The complexities faced by a heterogeneous nation where people of different races, religions, politics and ethnic origins live, work, walk, study, love, and play side-by-side are better understood and accommodated when our best and most original thinkers are able to give us insight into the workings and potential problems of all cultures. The political and social roles of intellectuals must not be minimized. I offer the following encouragement to young Black men and women who would enter their ranks. Be forever visionary, yet practical, empirical and productive, tough-skinned, strong egoed, with critical minds that challenge ignorance in the face of deep fear. Likewise, be steadfast in the following:

1. Question authority, especially that of the state and of national, international and transnational corporations.
2. Do not easily accept conventional wisdom, history or politics.
3. Always look beyond one's own culture and history to be able to examine not only the local situation but in order to see the larger picture of which the average citizen may not be aware.

4. Love the confrontation within the analysis of ideas-those agreed with, at odds with and foreign to ones' own experience.

5. Be willing and strong enough to go public with the truth, especially when that truth is unpopular, unconventional and not in the best interest of "big" people.

6. Be active in sharing liberal ideas of freedom, democracy, justice, healthcare and education for all, and especially for women and ethnic groups not in the majority.

7. Be willing to share personal resources. Find available resources and spend quality time among the less fortunate and needy of ones' community and the world doing intellectual and intelligent work.

8. Be careful of the corrupting powers of money, fame, status, wealth, sex, power and the false assessment of one's own importance (i.e., the Afrocentric or Eurocentric ego).

9. Be in the forefront of creating, building and maintaining independent Black institutions—especially in the areas of education and community such as schools, libraries, publising companies and mass media.

No society or people can develop or advance without serious financial and institutional support of their intellectuals. Intellectuals involved in research need quality time to think deeply, study rigorously, plan carefully and act in the best interest of themselves and their people. People who challenge the obvious, question the accepted, avoid easy answers and conclusions, travel to the unknown recesses of the mind, spirit and the universe often live next door. These people are a gift to us, we need to make a place at the table for them, especially those who are Black, brown and women; those persons who have been systematically locked out because of their race, gender or ethnic origins.

However, I must interject that all intellectual work is not good, pure or just. The experimental work done on enslaved people and prisoners, the Nazis use of imprisoned Jews and others, the Tuskegee experiment on Black men and others in the U.S. are not to be forgotten, negated or minimized. Scientific racism nurtured receptive minds in the West and is still an undercurrent belief among many intellectuals. These men and some women abused their privileged station and used their minds to actively support the small and evil minded people in this world. True intellectuals will always rise above the limited expectations of others, and most of them understand that freedom in its most precious definition means respect and opportunity for all. There is nothing like a young mind on fire, regardless of from where she or he comes. Part of the most important work of intellectuals should be to work with and inspire the nation's young people.

Of course, this will not be done if the nation's most important and productive intellectuals join the forces of money, privilege and academic exclusivity. If our best minds approached the problems of the nation's public schools like they seek funding and work from the Pentagon and transnational corporations we'd probably get a better return on our taxes and a more informed and active citizenry. As such, the best of our intellectuals must consider some pro-bono work for the public interest, especially the Black public interests, which at the core of any solution helps the entire nation. However, intellectuals at Black colleges, universities and institutions are generally overworked, underpaid, not always appreciated and not given the support or encouragement that their colleagues receive at white institutions. This environment at Black institutions must change if we are to keep and nurture our best minds. Finally, do not lose optimism and idealism. Most importantly, remember the advantages or disadvantages of your own childhood as you grow and make advances in your work and always remember that the great majority of the world's population is poor and most children go to bed hungry each night. If our best intellectuals were about solving this and like problems, this indeed, would be a much more promising world.

# III.

## WOMEN

We cannot effectively resist domination if our efforts to create meaningful, lasting personal and social change are not grounded in a love ethic...To give ourselves love, to love blackness, is to restore the true meaning of freedom, hope and possibility in all our lives.

—bell hooks
*Salvation: Black People and Love*

I can voice my ideas without hestitation or fear because I am speaking, finally, about myself. I am Black and I am female and I am a mother and I am bisexual and I am a nationalist and I am an anti-nationalist. And I mean to be fully and freely all that I am!

—June Jordan
*Technical Difficulties: African-American Notes on the State of the Union*

# Liberating Men About Liberating Women

No one among us should not feel pain in our hearts for the sexual oppression of young women and girls that occurs in all nations. We should all be outraged. But how does one shake loose a medieval consciousness? I say a consciousness because I truly believe that it is just that basic. Yes, I am aware that violence against women is historical, psychological and cultural at a mass level, but I am also aware that change often starts in one's mind, with one person at a time.

We live in a world where patriarchal leadership in most cultures is the norm; where a man—a father, a grandfather, a brother, an uncle or a son in a family, almost any family—rules. As a man, if you truly love the women folk of your families, you must ask yourself several critical questions. "Do I love, care for and respect the females of my family at the same deep level that I love, care for and respect the males of the family?" If the answer is yes, then the next question is "Am I willing to make the same and often greater commitment to the females of my family that I have made to the males? Am I willing to encourage them to reach for their dreams and to assist them to the best of my ability, in developing their minds, bodies and spirits, to assist them in nurturing their natural talents in a supportive family environment that is free, open and encouraging?" "Am I willing to be a vocal advocate of women's equality and liberation inside the family and publicly when I am with men and boys on the job, the basketball court, or in the clubs and centers of men's entertainment and power?"

Ignorance is contagious and breeds like overfed roaches in most rich, middle-class and impoverished communities. Outdated and nonfunctioning customs and traditions exist in most, if not all, cultures dominated by men. In far too many cultures women and children are still viewed as property to be put on the table of deals that guarantee for most of them a life of suffering, pain, unhappiness and servitude. The same must be said for the male-dominated hip-hop culture. These cultures must be questioned and, if necessary, confronted where ever they exist.

Whether the oppressive communities are religious, secular or a combination, their outright denial of women the equal protection under the law, as well as access to the institutions of intellectual development is truly a travesty. The Black church, as a primary spiritual center and the defining institutiuon of the Pan-African and Black Nation, must be in the forefront of redefinition and leadership in reference to Black women.

It is easy to publicly condemn the oppression of women on a grand scale, as in talking to the masses. However, such condemnation often falls on deaf ears unless coming from a powerful voice in government, the corporate world, religious community, or major academic institutions. And, when change is initiated it must be at a national policy level if it is to affect local customs and traditions that have guided the lives of women and men for centuries.

Young men, you must understand that it is, indeed, within your power to make significant social and cultural advances. However, change only starts when individuals operating within families, communities, block clubs, fraternities, institutions, cultures, etc. realize that certain actions within your culture, ethnic group or nation are out of step with progressive thought and development.

Each of us must first examine our own hearts, minds and actions toward women and girls. That is, as men in all of our relationships—personal and professional—do we accord the same regard to women that we give to men? Secondly, we must all question the status-quo. Just because "we've always done it that way" does not make it right, correct or good for the development of young men and women. To that end, I strongly recommend the following books to help you on the road to developing an intellectual basis for equality among the genders.

*Words of Fire* — Beverly Guy-Sheftall (editor)
*Focusing: Black Male-Female Relationships*
    — Delores P. Aldridge
*Black Women, Feminism and Liberation: Which Way?*
    — Vivian Gordon
*When and Where I Enter* — Paula Giddings

*Ain't I a Woman: Black Women and Feminism* — bell
	hooks
*Deals with the Devil and other Reasons to Riot*— Pearl
	Cleage
*Strategies for Resolving Conflicts in Black Male-Female
Relationships* — LaFrancis Rodgers-Rose
*The Black Feminist Reader* — T. Denean Sharpley-
	Whiting
*Technical Difficulties*—June Jordan
Any of the works of Alice Walker

These books are jump starts to open you up to a
whole new world of original Black thinkers on the question of gender equality. If you are truly ready for revolu-
tionary transformation, start here. And, always remember, stopping the women stops the future.

Young brothers, honor Black women because they
have carried the weight, baggage, criticism and nurtured
the children of our people and provided backbone to
our struggle when there were no other backs or bones.
Honoring of Black women is not some romantic illusion
about momma and grandmomma always being there to
heal a cold, fix a meal, keep the church open, provide
hard earned pennies and dollars for life sustaining essentials. No! Indeed, Black women did and continue to
clean their babies behinds, breast or bottle feed, educate
them and use their hands rather forcefully on their children's legs and butts when they (we) stray too far off
track. Black women have been our answers, no matter

the questions. They have been the period and exclamation points in our many paragraphs of life. Honor Black women because they are the "yes" and "can do" in the midst of crippling denials, mistaken visions, demeaning history in the politics and economy of illusion. Honor Black women because you understand and appreciate the sacrifices and commitments they made to be nurses, doctors, teachers, engineers, scientists, professors, lawyers, judges, university presidents, Ph.Ds, entrepreneurs, carpenters, policewomen, professional basketball players, tennis players, track and field athletes, artists, writers, poets, wives, mothers and good and productive women. Honor Black women because simply put, we Black men would not be here if they had not said yes to Black families. That commitment fundamentally is the first and most lasting fact of our reality.

> The women are colors of earth and ocean
> earth as life,
> the beginning waters
> magnificent energy.
> as the women go, so go the people
> determining mission
> determining possibilities.
> stopping the women stops the future.
>
> without great teachings,
> without important thoughts,
> without significant deeds,

the ordinary emerges as accepted example
gluing the women to kitchens,
afternoon soaps,
and the limiting imagination of sightless men.
producing a people that move with the
quickness of decapitated bodies
while
calling such movement                    .
divine.

possibilities:  listen to the mind of women, the voices of big mama, zora neale, sister nora, fanny lou,
pretty renee, gwen brooks, queen nzinga, and warrior mothers.   all birth and prophecy, black and
heart warm, bare and precise. the women detailing
the coming collapse or rise.  the best and best of
youth emerging. telling triumphantly. if we listen, if
we feel & prepare.

# Rape:
## The Need for an Anti-Rape Culture

As I write this, three Black men in Chicago have been arrested and charged with the murder of a twenty-seven year old Black woman. DNA evidence linked the three men to the rape and death of La Cressha Avery. According to an assistant Cook County State's Attorney of Illinois, as reported in the *Chicago Sun-Times* (September 19, 2000), the three men allegedly "dragged her inside the first floor vacant apartment, where they raped her and strangled her, wrapped her in a blanket and threw her through the back window."

This is not an isolated incident in this country or the Black community. The rape of Black women by Black men or any men is a cancer and is a growing concern in most Black communities. Rape is the violation and negation of the spirit, soul and physical presence of women. This attitude toward women is taught to us early in our lives and the best way to combat it is to adapt zero tolerance against any mistreatment of women and children. This would include sexual harassment, verbal abuse, any activity that could lead to the sexual and physical abuse of women and children.

As part of the definition of new men or manhood, I would encourage the absolute respect and support of women to be at the top of the list. Remember these women are our mothers, sisters, grandmothers, aunts, wives, daughters, close relatives, friends and lovers. Obviously, new education is required here which must be ongoing in all families, religious centers, male bonding groups, educational institutions and the workplace. I would encourage young men to start by reading *Surviving the Silence: Black Women's Stories of Rape* by Charlotte Pierce-Baker, a heart wrenching book about Black women revealing their souls and hearts to us about their horrible experiences of rape.

There are few human acts more negating of the human spirit than rape. The most cowardly and dastardly act against women is rape. Rape is a clear indication that a culture or civilization is out of control. Men and boys who wish to become real men do not singularly or as a group rape women, or men, under any circumstances. In fact, conscientious whole men are anti-rapist in thought, principles and actions. An anti-rapist male will use all of his strength, heart and soul that he can muster to prevent rape, those that are about to begin and those in progress. Rape prevention starts early with the proper education of boys and girls. Being an anti-rapist is not hard or difficult work, it is right work, it is moral and ethical work. It is work starting with the intelligent cultivation and nurturing of men who possess an undying love for life as well as respect for their mothers, grandmothers, sisters, aunts, women relatives and friends, wives, daughters and by extension all women regardless of race, class, religion or ethnic identity.

I will offer twelve strategies that if incorporated will drastically reduce and/or end rape.

1. It is your responsibility to be anti-rapist; you must be counter-rapist in thought, conversations, raps, organizations, and actions.
2. Understand that being a counter-rapist is honorable, manly, and necessary for a just society.
3. Understand that anti-rapist actions are part of the Black tradition; being an anti-rapist is in keeping with the best of African culture, family and extended family configurations. Even in times of war, many men were known to honor and respect the personhood of children and women.
4. Be glowing examples of men who are fighting to treat women as equals. Be fair and just in your associations with women. Families as now defined and constructed must continually be re-assessed. In today's economy most women, married and unmarried, must work. We men must encourage women in their work and must be intimately involved with housework and the rearing of children.
5. Teach your daughters how to defend themselves and maintain an uncompromising stance toward men and boys.
6. Try to understand that just as men are different from one another, women also differ; therefore we must try to not stereotype women into the limiting and often debilitating expectations of men. We must

encourage and support them in their searching and development.

7. Be unafraid and supportive of independent, intelligent and self-reliant women. And by extension, understand that intelligent women think for themselves and may not want to have sex with a particular man. This is a woman's prerogative.

8. Be bold and strong enough to stop other men (relatives, friends, or strangers) from raping and to intervene in a rape-in-progress with the fury and destruction of a hurricane against the rapist.

9. Listen to women. Listen to women, especially to womanist/feminist/Pan-Africanist philosophies of life. Also, study the writings of women, especially Black women.

10. Act responsibly to the listening and studying. Be a part of and support anti-rape groups for boys and men. Introduce anti-rape discussion into men's groups and organizations.

11. Never stop growing. Understand that growth is limited and limiting without the input of intelligent women.

12. Learn to love. Study love. Even if one is at war, if there is to be a sane and livable world, love and respect, respect and love, must conquer. Rape is anti-love, anti-respect. Love is not easy. One does not fall in love but grows into love.

We can put to rest the rape problem in one generation if its eradication is as important to us as our cars, jobs, careers, sport-games, beer, and quest for power.

# WHO WILL MY
# DAUGHTERS MARRY?

Notice that I frame the title of this short essay in its active voice. It is not who will marry my daughters. My daughters Mariama and Laini are not victims. They are young women in their twenties who are the products of a loving and knowledge based up-bringing, nurtured and tutored in the best elementary, secondary schools and colleges possible. They were raised in culturally sensitive homes by parents who loved them and were committed to their future like water and oxygen are to life. Their parents were/are political and cultural activists and educators. My daughters did not have to find their identities as women of African ancestry; they were born into it naturally. Blackness to them was not bad weather or images of a misunderstood and ravished continent, but fresh juice; drum-voices of ancient music filled their young souls and sprits with possibilities of "can do." We believe in Black families and the fundamental power of love, struggle and spiritual attainment.

My daughters are also daughters and sisters of Spelman College under the presidency of Dr. Johnetta B. Cole. They were taught by and experienced the powerful presence of Dr. Beverly Guy-Sheftall and others, and therefore have a healthy, strong and wondrous sense of themselves as Black women wrapped in a superior education. Their college education seldom contradicted their earlier examples. It confirmed and built upon that which they knew to be true; to be female and Black is a definition in itself, worthy of study, reflection, development, empowerment and respect. Spelman crowned my daughters and others who listened and learned with an inner power and peace that easily separated them from the unsuspecting Black majority of young women and men who populate this nation. They found their voices in themselves as a result of studying the lives of the significant women who preceded them and upon whose shoulders they, and we, stand.

Both of my daughters are highly intelligent, cultured, beautiful, talented, tall, spiritual, confident, hard workers, articulate, well traveled, curious, readers—and women who know what they want to do with their lives. They are well mannered, not elitist, and do not suffer foolish young men or old men easily. This is not to deny that they are fun to be with, smile and laugh often as young people should. They do silly things, make poor choices in friends and lovers, live to buy clothes and shoes, are not the worst cooks or homemakers, but are always clean, somewhat frugal with their money and intimately aware and conscious of people less fortunate than they are.

Mariama lives in New Haven, Connecticut, has taught in public middle school and is directing a young people's organization while completing a Masters' degree in History and Africana Studies at Cornell University. Laini lives in New York and is a journalist, writer and producer at a major dot com website. Just as their mothers (both Ph.Ds from the University of Chicago), they are professional and progressive women. They are African-centered and community-based in theory and actions and come from homes where women's liberation was studied, discussed and practiced. They are looking for Black men to be friends, possible lovers and mates who have more on their minds than sex, football, sex, basketball, running the streets, getting over, woo, playing games, sex, Afrocentric egos, male violence, booty call, player clubs, being a millionaire by thirty, sex, new and traditonal ways of getting high and looking for women to mother or take care of them while supplying unlimited sex.

My daughters are seeking male friends and associates who will rise above the limiting ideas and expectations of their fathers, grandfathers, great-grandfathers and the woman restricted cultures of this nation and the world. Their standards require that they be accepted and acknowledged as no less than equal at all levels of human involvement. As new women building on the tradition of those who led the way, they will not be an afterthought to be consulted after the choices have been made, after the decisions are confirmed and the money and positons allocated. Gender equality, like human rights, is not modern paper talk, is not a reward given to smart women or good "girls" by enlightened men. Gender equality is a hard fought right, earned by women and men who are not afraid of their own shadows, mistakes and history. Changing the political, economic and cultural status of women has pushed people from all cultures to risk their lives, property, spirit and sanity to confront antiquated and backward systems, laws and practices created by evil men, good men, and most certianly by ignorant men.

The world is not just when it comes to gender and race issues in the United States. If we are not in on determining the language to be used or how the money is to be spent, it is all but guaranteed that we'll be tap-dancing to other people's melodies and working at slave wages in the offices, factories, sweatshops and fields of men whose only concerns are for their immediate families, ethnic groups and the making of super profits. My daughters, as well as the daughters of others, deserve a fighting chance at life, love and family. My concern as a father is where are the young Black men ready for the challenge of my daughters and young women like them?

## Believe in Marriage

The strengths of any people are reflected in their institutions. The foundation of all nations can be measured by the stability of their families, the smallest and-most important of institutions. The weakness of any people can be traced to their bonding traditions and the treatment of women and girls. Marriage as a common practice that is observed, maintained, honored and encouraged in all nations is one institution that must not be taken for granted.

In the West, when two people commit to each other and pledge a life together, their responsibility in such an act is not only for themselves, their families, and communities, but most importantly it is for the children that will surely come as a result of their love and traditions. This is why it is absolutely necessary that young people are carefully counciled, mentored and instructed on the demands and responsibilities of marriage. All people are not made for marriage, all people are not made for parenthood. Children should not be, must not be accidents. No child is illegitimate or should be unwanted. This is a large concern in a culture that has all but given up on young men who somehow feel free to drop their seeds any and everywhere and not feel any responsibility for the love, upbringing, education and security of their children. If this book means anything it's that being a man or woman is much more than making babies. Quality manhood starts with accepting the responsibility of fatherhood. A part of being an adult is learning to stand by one's decisions, and the decision to have unprotected sex often leads to unprotected children. This must change.

There are too many unloved and unprotected children in the United States and a very large percentage of them are Black. All of our institutuions must immediately demand that Black men acknowledge and accept responsibility for their children. Also, Black women must be taught to make better choices in their love lives.

This is not easy because there are few human acts as difficult and deceptive as young "love." The complexity of the human heart in relationship to another is often compromised and all too often when others can notice a mismatch the involved couple only sees pleasure, "love" and promises.

Having been married for twenty-eight years, I can state in no uncertain terms that it has been and is the most important and uplifting experience in my life. Not only because of our children, but marriage brought stabilty, shared vision, an intellectual lover and partner and an understanding of Black women that only deep love and respect can bring.

Finally, we must stand up for and shout loud and clear that marriage between the "right" people is not only necessary but encouraged. Also, where marriage is not a solution or workable, and if children are involved, that the "brothers" must be commited for life to the healthy development of their children. Anything less is unacceptable.

# One Hundred Reasons To Believe In Women's Liberation

Gwendolyn Brooks, Margaret G. Burroughs, Safisha Madhubuti, Shirley Graham DuBois, Mary McLeod Bethune, Barbara A. Sizemore, Rosa Parks, Margaret Walker Alexander, Darlene Clark Hine, Betty Carter, Geneva Smitherman, Mari Evans, Lucille Clifton, Gayle Jones, Alice Walker, Elizabeth Catlett, Harriet Tubman, Johari Amini Hudson, Anita Hill, Thulani Davis, Arundhati Roy, Patricia J. Williams, Toni Morrison, Aretha Franklin, Maxine Graves, Betty Shabazz, Toni Cade Bambara, Judy Richardson, Delores P. Aldridge, Anna Julia Cooper, Sonia Sanchez, Beverly Guy-Sheftall, Johnnetta B. Cole, Diane Nash, Nina Simone, Sandra E. Gibbs, Coretta Scott King, Octavia Butler, Frances Cutis Frazier, Inez Hall, Susan L. Taylor, Cynthia Cooper, Pearl Cleage, Nikki Giovanni, Maya Angelou, Assata Shakur, Naomi Long Madgett, Audre Lorde, Wilma Rudolph, WNBA, Willalyn Fox, Myrlie Evers, Charshee McIntyre, Jayne Cortez, Erykah Badu, Ella Baker, Laini Mataka, Marita Golden, Cicely Tyson, Sweet Honey In The Rock, Val Gray Ward, June Jordan, Queen Mother Moore, bell hooks, Ruby Dee, Lolita Green, Gloria Joseph, Sherley Ann Williams, Zora Neale Hurston, Vivian V. Gordon, Abena Joan Brown, Mary Church Terrell, Estella Conwill Majozo, Andrea L. Taylor, Ida Wells-Barnett, Julie Dash,

Eleanor Traylor, Angela Jackson, Dorothy Irene Height, Joycelyn Elders, Frances Cress Welsing, Katherine Dunham, Angela Davis, Mariama Richards, Laini N. Madhubuti, Janet Hutchinson-Lee, Winnie Mandela, Kimya Moyo, Lorraine Hansberry, Madam C.J. Walker, Marimba Ani, Msiba Ann Grundy, Bessie Head, Julianne Malveaux, Julia Hare, the unknown women.

Are you aware of and understand the wonderment and power of these women? Do you believe that your life has been enriched as a result of their work and their presence among us? Can you walk and communicate with these women without fear? Do you believe that most women have the capacity for greatness in them? Do you believe that your mother, sister, grandmothers, aunts, female relatives and friends have received the nurturing and education necessary to fulfill their dreams? Do the Black men that you associate with have any knowledge of these women? Do you really believe that all women should be able to fight for their dreams, enjoy equal rights and have open doors to institutions that can assist them in achieving their potential? Are you afraid of intelligent, assertive, beautiful, athletic, culturally focused and highly competent women? If you can answer positively to the above questions, believe in the power of women and plan to act in the affirmative toward them, please sign here:

_____

Now start your own list. Put your mother at the top of the list, even if you do not know who she is.

# IV.

## PROGRESSIVE NURTURING: THE SAVING GRACE

African American people need an African-centered peda-
gogy because racism and worldwide Eurocentric hegemonic
attitudes and practices are still the order of the day.

—Safisha Madhubuti
*African-centered Education*

...raising (children) is "providing for," while rearing is "responding to." Raising can be satisfied by providing the essentials: food, shel-
ter, clothing and reasonable care. "Rearing" is a crefully thought out
process. Rearing begins with a goal and is supported by a clear view of
what are facts and what is truth (and the two are not necessarily synonymous). Rearing is complex and requires scrifice and dedication. It
is an ongoing process of "preparation." Joe Kennedy reared presidents;
the British royal family rears heirs to the English throne; and when a
young African doctor, born in the contintent and presently in self-exile
in a neighboring country because of her ANC (African National
Congress) commitment as interviewed on the news recently and was
asked if she was not afraid for her four-year-old son, given her political
activism, said, "He has a duty to lay down his life for his people. He is
my son, but he is also the son of an oppressed people," she announced
the rearing of a "race man." ....Obviously something different, some
carefully thought out process, some long-range political view is present
when one has a clear sense of one's own reality and therefore intends
to rear presidents, rulers, or free men and women.

—Mari Evans
*How We Speak*

# Children First

As I travel the country lecturing at the nations colleges, churches and community centers, young brothers often ask, "How do you maintain your spirit?" They are surprised at the energy, optimism and hope for the future of a Black man at the ripe age of fifty-nine. In a world where we are bombarded daily with news of impending doom—whether it's genocide in Rwanda, ethnic cleansing in Kosovo, earthquakes in Turkey and India, floods in South America, the hourly drive-by shootings in urban America or the tragedy of 9/11/2001— too often a climate of doubt exists among many young Black men who must make their way in a world they don't completely understand.

I credit my outlook to several things. I have a family, wife, five children, a mother-in-law and adopted mothers whom I love dearly. I have an extended family whom I equally love of relatives, cultural children and friends who see each day as a joyous challenge. For most of my adult life I have been involved in political and cultural struggles. I have founded or co-founded publishing companies, schools, bookstores, political initiatives, writers conferences and retreats, cultural centers and institutes at private and public universities. I have been involved in close to forty years of struggle—with successful and failed political and cultural movements and have learned and absorbed many lessons that are not taught in any classroom. But more than anything else, that which has brought daily joy to my life has been my continued interaction with children and young people.

Outside of parenting my/our children, few things are more important to me than growing and mentoring our two schools in Chicago—New Concept School (an independent pre-school) and Betty Shabazz International Charter School (the African-Centered elementary school of Chicago Public Schools). I walk the halls of our schools regularly. The spirit in a child's uninhibited smile or laughter does much more for me than any vitamins or herbs. Seeing, touching, listening to and being around the energy and spirit of young children is like water to crops, the sun on a winter's cold face or "yes" to unknown tomorrows. A child's smile is like a magnet. Children's innocent, open minds and deep need of family love and support is the reason that loving and responsible parents and adults must be in their lives. Talented, skilled, loving and committed teachers should be in their classrooms. Most children, regardless of race, religion, gender, culture or national origin come out of their mothers' body at genius level. The family, culture, and nation that they are born into can either work hard to develop the genius in them do nothing or very little, which aids in knocking them off the genius track before the age of five.

From birth, our children must be viewed as potential geniuses. We must accept the fact of their young brilliance and be prepared to nurture them by providing the structures—spiritual, educational, cultural, political and financial that confirm their gifts. If we give them an equal chance to grow and succeed in a world that is not fair or child-centered, their "yeses" will not become disappointed and destructive "nos."

I love children and have been around my own and others long enough to realize one undeniable fact—if given love, children love unconditionally. However, if we fail in our love, most children will shut down and most intellectual development stagnates or slows considerably. We must protect and nurture their young love. We can show our love for them through "right" and developmental acts that encourage them to become more than they and others believe that they can become. To the best of our abilities we must be fired up mothers, fathers and teachers, ready to give our children the head start they require in a difficult, confusing and dangerous world.

If you find that your life and work is not feeding your spirit or giving you the satisfaction that makes you a whole and loving person, find a program with children in it and volunteer some quality time. Give our children the best that we have to offer and fewer of our elders will end up in nursing homes waiting and hoping to die quickly and of course, alone.

To this beautiful goal I strongly suggest a number of strategies:

1. Learn early the importance of touching your children in a loving and fatherly manner. The mother's bond is almost immediate upon birth. Be there with your wife/mate at birth. Hold and kiss your baby as soon as possible. If possible be in the bed with your wife/mate at birth as your child comes out of his/her mother's womb. Request that you be able to cut the umbilical cord and be active in the birthing process.

2. From the very beginning be a participant in the parenting of your children. From the preparation of their living space to the acquisition of clothes, toys, books, food and other essentials. A mother's response is intuitive, her bonding is both biological and cultural. Men have to be taught, encouraged and motivated to be more than bystanders in our children's lives. It is a wonderful and civilizing act to be a nurturer in the lives of our children as well as a provider.

3. Remember that young minds start developing before birth, most certainly once conception is confirmed. To have intelligent children, we must not only love them unconditionally, but create an environment that nurtures and grows their/your minds. All or most of their life activities must be to this end; making them intelligent, inquisitive, happy, well-rounded, culturally and physically strong, and loving children, teenagers and adults.

4. Do not just rely on your own upbringing as the only guide, study the current literature on progressive

parenting while keeping responsible elders involved. Most libraries and bookstores have entire sections devoted to parenting.

5. Do not let the television, CD player, computers or any other electronic plaything become your children's babysitters. Children need quality time, in meaningful activities with their fathers, mothers and grandparents. And, when the electronic world is allowed into your children's lives, control it. If you don't, it will control and guide them.

6. As soon as possible involve them in organized activity with other like-minded children such as art and music classes, sports and outdoor play activities, etc.

7. Use weekends to take them to the many cultural activities in urban areas. This world includes but is not limited to theatre, museums, story hours at libraries, bookstores, and live music. Sports outings are also excellent family entertainment.

8. Take family vacations. Drive to national parks. Visit other cities in your region.

9. Be pro-active in your own intellectual development, whether formal or informal. If your children see you reading and studying, they will want to do the same thing. Build a home library where books are used in a natual and developmental way. Start early—reading to your children. Take your children to public libraries weekly.

10. Hug and kiss them in the morning and before bed

every day. Tell them often how much you love them and often confirm the beauty of their skin and the intelligence of their young minds.

Remember that you as a brother, father, uncle or grandfather represent more than just a male body in the latest clothes of the day. Your space of influence is much greater than you realize. The way you articulate your thoughts to the very way you walk, study, love, live, truth-talk, dance and talk in the world around you is absorbed by the children and young people in your life. You are, indeed, an example even if you wish not to be one. If you attack life with a love passion and genuinely understand the large challenges before you, then and only then will you grow as a man able to confirm his place in the world while claiming ownship of said place. Confronting, accepting and overcoming all of life's tests builds character. Finally, we want our children and young people to be better than us. For them to acheive, acheivement needs to be in their young lives. We cannot be just drive-by parents, teachers, mentors or big brothers; there is too much at stake here and all of us are integral to the success of the whole.

# ART:
## Nurturing Exceptional Children

Civilization, the act of building a civil and enlightened community, starts with the comprehensive education of the smallest among us, our children. Civility begins with an enlightened way of speaking the many expressions of culture, truth, love and life enhancing possibilities. This is almost always ushered in with a resonant sunrise smile—as in its great to be alive! And then, slowly at first comes the reasons, the whys, the ins and outs and eventually the logic of what a good life is, starting with babies first hearing their mother's heartbeat and as soon as reasonably possible the father's loving voice.

The heartbeat grows and glows with the music of Art Blakey's Jazz Messengers and the spirituals of Mahalia Jackson. That is, at birth great Black music, the Nat King Coles, Charlie Parkers and Billie Holidays of the world should be playing quietly in the delivery and recovery spaces of the babies' birth. Then, take the infant home to a house showered in the visual voices and images of Margaret Burroughs, Elizabeth Catlett, Charles White, Jeff Donaldson, Richard Hunt, and other favorite likenesses of the family; also, be sure that the colors of their tradition greets them at the door, the African rainbow where Black is the border and the earth tones of brown, green, yellow and orange play sweet melody to the babies' new eyes.

At feeding time—whether breast or bottle—try playing the recorded poetry of Gwendolyn Brooks, Langston Hughes, Margaret Walker, Robert Hayden, Sterling Brown and others letting the words slowly etch themselves onto the memory of the newborn. At bed time immediately start reading the children stories of Sharon Bell Mathis, Eloise Greenfield, Julius Lester, Virginia Hamilton, Muriel Feelings as well as the tales from their families' history. Make sure that in the best places in your home there are bunches of family, extended family and best friends' photographs interspersed with the black/white and colored photos of Gordon Parks, James Van Derzee, Jeanne Montonssamly-Ashe, Chester Higgins Jr., Roy Lewis, Fern Logan, Roy DeCarava and Roland L. Freeman.

Try your hardest in the first five years of life to introduce your children to live music, dance and theatres of the African, Asian, European and American worlds. Introduce them to the alphabet, numbers and the community in which they live. Before the age of six, think seriously about giving them music and/or art lessons which should naturally grow out of their viewing the creativeness of their own surroundings and daily listening to Duke Ellington, Aretha Franklin, Louis Armstrong, Terry Collier, Eryka Badu, the Dells and the thousands of other musicians from Black culture and others.

The identity secret or "Who am I" question is answered in the act of discovery, finding the know in knowing. All children should be deeply loved and naturally washed, dried, showered, rinsed, toweled and gently sunned, taught and confirmed in the essential creative expressions of their people. Art defines, expands and signifies meaning while germinating gigantic hope. Art is a prodigious and primary energy force. Children's active participation in music, dance, painting, poetry, film, photography and the indigenous crafts of their people is what makes them whole, significantly human, secure in their own skin, culture and abilities. Thus, generating in them unlimited possibilities.

Art is fundamental instruction and food for a people's soul as they translate the many languages and acts of becoming, often telling them in no uncertain terms that all humans are not pure or perfect. However, the children of all cultures inherit their creators' capacity to originate from the bone of their imaginations the closest manifestations of purity, perfection and beauty, art. Art at its best encourages us to walk on water, dance on top of trees and skip from star to star without being able to swim, keep a beat or fly. A child's "on fire" imagination is the one universal prerequisite for becoming an artist:

Magnify your children's mind with art,
jumpstart their questions with art,
introduce your children to the cultures of the world
     through art,
energize their young feet, spirits and souls with art,
infuse the values important to civil culture via art,
keep them curious, political and creative with art,

speak and define the universal language of
    beauty with art,
learn to appreciate peace with art,
approach the cultures of others through their art,
introduce the spiritual paths of other
    people through their art.
keep young people in school, off drugs and
    out of prison with art,
keep their young minds running, jumping
    and excited with art.
examine the nurturing moments of love,
    peace and connecting differences with art

Art allows and encourages the love of self and others. The best artists are not mass murderers, criminals or child molesters, they are in the beauty and creation business. Art is elemental to intelligent intelligence, working democracy, freedom, equality and justice. Art, if used wisely and widely, early and often is an answer and a question. It is the cultural lake that the indigenous rivers of dance, music, local images and voices flow. Art is the waterfall of life, reflecting the untimely and unique soul of a people. Art is the drumbeat of good and great hearts forever seeking peace and a grand future for all enlightened peoples. For these are the people the world over who lovingly proclaim, "give the artist some," kind words, financial support, yeses from your heart,  knowing intuitively that there will be creative reciprocity in all that they give us. Why? Because fundamentally art inspires, informs, directs, generates hope and challenges the receiver to respond. And finally, and this is consequential, the quality of the art determines the quality of the responses.

# PRISON:
## Keeping Our Sons Home

There are about one and a half million Black, Latino and poor white men locked up in the nation's prisons. Two-thirds are Black. Many are there because they have committed serious crimes against society. Some are there because they did not have competent legal representation. A very large percentage are there on drug related crimes—serving mandatory sentences for first time offenses. A great many more were caught in the wrong place at the wrong time.

Prison is not a beautiful place. It is a place of punishment and isolation from family, friends and loved ones. Prisons are brutal and even a short stay will test every fiber in one's body. I used to visit prisoners rather regularly until the sea of young, Black and Latino men got to me. There are few things more painful than seeing young bright, intelligent and mostly poor men caught in a system they know little about.

Most of these young men never had a chance, coming out of urban America with a "jones" up their nose and a big chip on their young shoulders. Most of them never learned to ask for help and had few if any loving adults to guide them. The unifying horror stories in their young lives is that many of them never outgrew the trauma of coming into manhood/adulthood without fathers and/or father-like men in their lives to give them much needed love, examples and responsible direction.

Prison construction is big business in America. States like Texas and California have very large and complex systems. Some states have privatized units to outside companies that have little knowledge in the field of correction. Most prisons are located long distances from urban areas, where most of the inmates are from, thus putting an extra burden on families to visit and maintain the necessary family and physical contact.

For poor people, the legal system is seldom fair and rarely operates in their interest. In the 1990s, in the United States over seventy-six men were released as a result of new evidence—primarily DNA. These men should have never been locked up. They and many others, because of their lack of wealth, were forced to rely on public defenders. As a result of their incarceration, their lives and that of their families have been altered and impacted upon negatively for at least the near future.

In order to avoid this dead-end situation, young boys and men—before falling through the cracks—must find productive communities of which to be a part. Obviously, the family is the first line of defense for keeping boys out of prison. Here, mothers are important, but fathers play a key role. Story after story of young prisoners reveal time missed with loving, caring and responsible fathers. Good fathers are imperative in the lives of sons. Boys approaching the teen years in urban America need strong and dependable fathers to help guide them through the land mines of gangs, drugs, poor schools, street based cultures and the thousands of other temptations that daily stop the healthy growth of young boys and men.

In the past, I've argued for African-centered boot camps for Black teenagers and young adults caught in the destructive cycle of the streets, courts, prisons, release and re-entry again through the same non-productive and non-responsive systems. I still recognize the need for this type of intervention. However, something needs to be done before young Black men become caught-up in this cycle.

There are groups of men in our community, retired and active non-commissioned officers (NCOs), high school and college/university sport coaches who, if called upon in an organized manner and asked to aid in saving and developing young boys, will respond in a favorable way. Often these men, due to their formal and informal education and training have positively impacted some of our most emotionally and physically abused youth. In many cases, the best NCOs and coaches remain the first "real" men and/or surrogate fathers to the fatherless. These men must begin to incorporate their skills and knowledge into an institutional framework or structure that would impact and influence young men in need, both before it is too late, as well as during the rehabilitation stage.

Some of the main elements missing in the lives of these young men should be at the heart of such organizations and include the following:

1. A family of older caring men who are respected in the larger Black community.
2. A sense of and an understanding of a disciplined life that is required to excel in the above ground world. This world includes knowledge of an acceptance of regular work (any kind) and an understanding of the importance of a work ethic.
3. An appreciation of, and respect for, the culture of their people, especially its history, art and political struggles.
4. A feeling of deep accomplishment as a result of real production in the above ground economy that is based upon accepted skills and knowledge that are respected by all people.
5. A relationship with a good lawyer. Read Christian Parenti's *Lockdown America: Police and Prisons in the Age of Crisis*, the most current and most insightful analysis of prisons and the people they impact the most.

The idea is that these young men, our sons, need an entirely new environment and culture that will encourage and enable them to reach their potential. An association with men who have accomplished a great deal in their lives will hopefully stimulate these young men in a way that they have not ever experienced. There is much more to this but most certainly these young men need to be situated in a caring, loving community that doesn't celebrate failure and considers success as the major option for young men who, for whatever reason, have been systematically locked out and locked-up. If our generation fails to build the groups, organizations, communities, and institutions, your generation, which has felt the trauma of prison firsthand must, must, must see this as a priority. This is one of your most important challenges.

# FATHERS AND SONS:
## The Healing Call

Each generation produces its own Griots—today's rappers and hip-hoppers. Young people who see too much too early, see the underside of bad breath and lies as their young minds are honoring the fires of idealism. Regardless of how strong or clear their message, it does not change the fact that boys need fathers. Tupac needed a loving daddy to check him, to curb his language, actions and aspirations. Biggie Smalls needed a baba to set parameters for him, to set goals larger than bodies draped in gold, diamonds and bitch-talk. Tupac and Biggie needed responsible fathers and elder men in their lives who loved them enough to challenge the streets and corners in them. They needed conscientious, caring men to tattoo their history and spirit on them like the dried ink that now rots on their dead bodies.

Sons nation-wide cry for love and guidance from fathers, grandfathers, adopted and cultural fathers. Their cries are tearless and muted, fearing the macho cat calls of peers caught in the same zoo of trapped boys seeking instruction, death-spirit and examples from older boys who dance to two laws: staying alive and getting over. Without life affirming love, art and actions, without supervised discipline and study, without loud examples of "can-do/must-do" possibilities and daily diets of father-love vitamins, Tupacs and Biggies will multiply.

137

And the word on the street is, "you ain't seen nothin, yet." A refresing analysis of the forces directing today's youth is Bakari Kitwana's *The Hip-Hop Generation* (2002).

This call is to the fatherless nation, hip-hop and no hop, church and church-less boys of genius who have never experienced a hug or a kiss from a man, never been loved as only fathers can love. This is a call to the men who drop seeds of life in women as if that is all life is about. This is a call to rappers and the rap-less, the boys with perpetual anger in their eyes, who wear gold and silver (often decorating their mouths) rather than use it to work for them. This message is to the father-less nation of boys who never discovered smiles, laughter or the wholeness of possibilities, opportunities or a confirming wellness.

> we the men of twenty-four-seven        at dawn
> of Nat, Garvey, DuBois, Medgar, Malcolm and King,
> of swift tongues, fast hands and educated ears
> must rise to the answer        before dawn,
> we are the quiet in the fire of unforgiven streets,
> we are the hands beating the come home drums,
> we are the homes surrounded in father-love, yeses
>     & stopwatches,
> we are the poetic spirit making life worth living.
>
> this is our call,
> to boys who earned their names suffering spit & fist.

scale your dreams
avoid the dust of manufactured fairy tales,
bury evil choices and mandate a working truth,
unscar your todays with a loving advocacy of tomorrow,
trust the sun, moon, grass, blooming flowers and
clean      water,
defeat the devil's wars, burn the torturers play
pager,
write your own truths, herein lies the challenge:
how far will good go in this age of lotteries and
mega churches?
how far will justice travel in the breath of polluted
judges, priest, police, lawyer and politicians?
how far will peace advance in the rhetoric of
clowns?
what role will wisdom play in the desert of bogus
thought?
this is our call,
sponsor our sons, fill the emptiness in their questions,
this is our theology: defeat the devil's plans
answer the s.o.s., save our sons with f.o.c., fathers
on call,
we are sacred answers for the deserted hearts of
boys becoming men.

# Naming Your Children

Before naming your children, think of this. One's name is pre-introduction. Our names are our calling cards to strangers, friends and family. A name fixes an image in the minds of those to whom you are an unknown. Names like Willie, Mary Jane, L.T., Trey, or Bertha Mae tells us a great deal about the person and his or her background. Each of us has in our minds an image associated with each of these popular names of the Western world.

Naming children is not, or should not, be like naming cats and dogs or horses and pigs. Just as serious thought should have gone into the decision to have children, serious consideration should be given to naming them. A name cements us for life. Names are cultural and political. There are historical differences between the names Kwame and Joe. Nzinga and Janice play to our ears at different cultural frequencies.

Generally, people who are aware of and practice their own cultural directives name their children in keeping with the historical, linguistic and bonding traditions of their culture. If African American people were truly free and liberated and had all that goes with people in control of their own destiny, this would not be such a large question in our lives. Without the substances of an empowered people—land, businesses, self-knowledge, health care institutions, finance, industry, adequate employment, and a heartfelt cultural confirmation—we often blindly name our children after movie stars, favorite songs and dead presidents.

Liberated minds fuel liberating and empowering actions. One's worldview or political approach to self-ownership is determined by one's cultural education and one's name is the first introduction we receive of a person's identity. In the sixties, seventies and eighties our people made up bodacious names like La Keshia, Bo Bo, Ice T., Whoopie, Whatchamacallit, etc. Enough.

> your name
> tells us who you are
> where you come from,
> where you are going
> and
> who is going with you.
> your name
> is legitimatization of the past
> confirmation of the present
> and
> direction for the future.

# Health:
## Saying Yes to Life

For over thirty years I have been personally pursuing optimal health. I, like most people, grew up eating and enjoying the food of my culture. This consisted of lots of beans, bread, canned foods, chicken, ground beef, spaghetti, roast, dairy foods and sugar in all forms. Sugar as in Kool-Aid, ice cream, soda, cakes, candy and just about all processed foods. As I learned later, sugar was to be the most dangerous commodity for my body, just ahead of salt and milk related products.

By the age of twenty-seven it was unusual to ever see me without a handkerchief blowing my nose every five minutes or so. My body was always full of mucus, my eyes were always seriously watered up in the spring and fall of the year and when I ate certain "foods" they would put me to sleep or cause me to sneeze violently. The doctors I visited, and there were many, just continued to give me drugs that best "contained" my reaction—for an hour or so.

In 1969, I along with Jewel Latimore, (a co-founder of Third World Press), now known as Dr. Johari Amini Hudson, began to search for alternatives to our health problems. The literature existed but we had to search for and work to find materials that were both scientifically sound and practical. We began to seriously change our diets, first cutting out the consumption of red meats and chicken. Shortly after that I started eliminating all flesh from my meals. My health began to slowly improve but I still encountered nasal problems.

In the early seventies, I started a strict regimen of fresh vegetable juices and fruit juices everyday. I developed the habit of under eating and only eating small meals rather than stuffing myself two or three time a day. By 1977 I made the big jump and discontinued the use of dairy products: milk, ice cream, cheese and anything else that had any milk content. For me this move to becoming a vegan—a strict vegetarian who eats no animal or dairy products— helped me live an almost disease-free life. Along the way, I started practicing yoga, meditation and increased my exercise program to at least six days a week. I learned about the curative and preventive health properties of drinking at least a gallon of clean water a day, along with the absolute necessity for fasting and cleansing diets.

In the early eighties the "green" revolution was sweeping the country. As the research developed and health stores and restaurants multiplied, my ability to eat properly when I traveled helped a great deal in maintaining my health. My consumption of wheatgrass juice and mainly consuming raw vegetables and fruits at most meals has kept me relatively free of illness.

In the thirty years or so, since I have been on this regimen, I have only had one illness which required hospitalization. That was two years ago when my appendix was removed. Other than that, I strongly stand on this diet as superior to all others in maintaining optimal health. We are fortunate today to have many alternatives to traditional Western healthcare which has been based upon the curative paradigm rather than preventative. Nevertheless, as with any money-generating business the alternative health and organic food business has its hustlers and con people. Be careful.

Out of the thousands of books published each year on health, I have found four that have been valuable to me in my life of preventative health lifestyle. They are John Robbins *Diet for a New America*, Linda Rector Page's *Healthy Healing*, Eric Schlosser's *Fast Food Nation: The Downside of the All-American Meal* and Udo Erasmus' *Fats that Heal, Fats that Kill.*

### Druglessness: Part of the Answer

It is not enough for you, as an individual to just say "no" to drugs. Yes, it is the mandatory start, but you must be in a family, extended family, community and a culture that logically, yet lovingly, understands and accepts the futility and dangers of drugs. People, especially young people, must understand the contradiction in the culture where some drugs are legal and others illegal. We must be honest to the point of embarrassment in explaining how a high with alcohol is less debilitating and harmful than a high with another underground drug. Why are cigarettes acceptable, legal and encouraged, while marijuana comes too often with a prison term? The medical effects of smoking cigarettes kills hundreds of thousands in America every year and millions worldwide. The addictive traps of drugs, whether alcohol, cigarettes, marijuana, cocaine, heroin, Robitussin, Tylenol and the thousands of laboratory created stimulants that flood the commercials and the underground markets, are enough to fuel a multi-billion dollar industry. We do not live in a drugless culture. Young people must be able to differentiate among the good, the bad and the ugly.

Children must be educated and loved away from ever trying drugs. This is only possible in a family, extended family, community and a culture where the adults, parents, care-givers, teachers, heros, spiritual and political leaders accept the responsibility of being an example for our children. A loving and caring father, mother and grandparents showing, living and being the examples of a "no drugs" lifestyle is a thousand times more effective than verbalizing a lie or preaching "no drugs" to closed ears.

### AIDS: Let Your Big Head Do the Thinking

In 1991 in my book, *Black Men: Obsolete, Single, Dangerous?*, I wrote about AIDS and its coming destruction on a great many African people in Africa and elsewhere. The research then was incomplete, but what was known and is confirmed today is that AIDS is not a homosexual disease and its virus is almost one hundred percent deadly if persons contracting it are not treated quickly with the most advanced medicine.

The major transmitter of the AIDS virus is still sex and shared drug paraphernalia. Much of Africa is now being ravished with death and sickness caused by AIDS. The HIV virus, often denied by many and given other names by others to hide the shame felt by family and friends is now the major cause for death on the continent, outdistancing wars, accidents and death from other diseases. According to *Time Magazine* (February 12, 2001) seventy-nine percent of those who died of AIDS in 1999 were Africans. Find that issue of *Time* and read it and share it with your family and friends. Educate yourself and your loved ones. Like most diseases that are passed from person to person, AIDS can be contained and eradicated. The white gay community in the United States is an excellent example of a community controlling the disease.

Most certainly this requires for many a life style change and a commitment to life rather than quick unprotected pleasure. As men and women, we do have choices and it is critical and life affirming that we make the right decision, now!

## A Health Strategy

1. Study nutrition. Use your local libraries and health food stores to locate the most up-to-date information about health. The key is to move toward pre-

ventative health. That is to adopt a lifestyle or a way of life that allows and encourages you and your loved ones to experience your personal best and optimal health. Remember we are all different, even though there are many life habits that are good for us that we all share. Eat less and drink at least eight glasses of clean water a day. Find the nutrition that works best for you and remember, "You are what you eat."

2. Exercise every day. I suggest a combination of deep stretches (yoga, cardiovascular and strength building). I do at least an hour a day. This requires me to rise early because I find it best to work out before my day starts. Fight stress by starting with an understanding of your own body's limitations. A great deal of stress is brought on by acquiring too much debt and trying to be who you are not. Rather than buying into commericalism and other people's lives, work into smiles, humor, quiet times and peace. And remember there are few acts as important as quality *sleep*. Seven to eight hours a night goes a long way in a stressful world.

3. Live in a sharing and giving mode. Value yourself and others. Try to do good work with children and young people. Understand the importance of self-esteem, which is not just a feel-good philosophy of life. Do not be afraid to say thank you or to give credit to people who also do good work. Seek out new friendships and relationships that will encour-

age the best in you and in them. Be grateful for life and its many possibilities. Always seek new knowledge, learning is life-long. Remember that most people in the United States never take advantage of the free life enhancing and sustaining options in their communities: libraries, recreation centers, forest preserves, museums, adult education at community colleges and universities and much, much more. Try to associate with a caring community.

4. Eat right! Avoid fast foods. Eat small amounts rather than stuffing yourself at every meal. Take a good multiple vitamin and try fresh vegetable juices such as carrots, celery, green peppers and spinach. Fresh fruit juices are curative also. Remember to drink a minimum of eight glasses of clean water a day. Slow down and listen to your own heartbeat.

5. Just as we service our cars we need to service our bodies. The choice is between nourishing activating or toxic experiences. Eat anti-oxident-rich foods and use anti-oxident-rich herbs, such as fresh vegetables, fruits, grains, nuts, and beans and rosemary, sage, dill, mint, ginger and garlic.

6. Find a community that celebrates life and understands the critical importance of laughter and smiles, learning and sharing, wealth, Black culture and quiet time. Remember, if you are to perform at the optimal, your spiritual, mental, emotional and physical levels must be in a healing and developmental

mode at all times.

---

*Note: As with all health related suggestions, mine
are purely personal and not shared to influence the
reader in any way other than purely informational. It
has proven to be best for me. I strongly suggest before
you make any life altering decisions about your health
that you first consult a trusted doctor or professional
health care provider.*

# V.
## LIBERATION

It is not, I think, a question of when and how the white people will "free" the black and the red people. It is a condescension to believe that we have the power to do that. Until we have recognized in them the full strength and grace of their distinctive humanity we will be able to set no one free, for we will not be free ourselves. When we realize that they possess a knowledge for the lack of which we are incomplete and in pain, then the wound in our history will be healed. Then they will simply be free, among us—and so will we, among ouselves for the first time, and among them.

—Wendell Berry
*The Hidden Wound*

In the end I believe that faith in reason will prevail. But it will not happen automatically. Freedom under law is hard work. If rulers cannot be trusted with arbitrary power, it is up to citizens to raise their voices at injustice. The most important office in a democracy, Justice Louis Brandeis said, is the office of citizen.

—Anthony Lewis
Farewell Column, *New York Times*, 12-15-01

# LEADERSHIP IN A COMPLEX WORLD

If asked, who is the Jewish leader, the Irish leader, or the Italian, Chinese, Polish, Japanese and American leader, other than the president, few could give an informed answer. However, Black folks are continuously asked to name the one or two African American leaders. We are somehow expected to quickly give names of the most outspoken and visible spiritual and/or secular person(s) in the local or national arenas who speak truth to power. Generally, that person(s) is always in opposition to white leadership and politics and his or her expertise is limited to the areas of human rights. This is a small pool from which to draw and by definition negates the wealth of leadership in all the other areas that any whole people automatically draws from.

There cannot be one, two or three leaders for a people if that people are truly to be empowered and in control of their own destiny. For a people to maximize their own cultural and economic imperatives, leaders in all the life areas must be harvested. We too have competent men and women who have distinguished themselves in construction, agriculture, psychology, military, politics, academia, history, commerce, literature, law enforcement, technology, science and social work, but most people are more aware of Black sport and entertainment leaders because of mass media.

In any democratic country, leadership is passed from generation to generation and is not confined to any one family or group. A person is generally not an active leader for life (except in some religious and educational traditions), because the wise of any people realize that the demands of leadership require the continued introduction of new faces, regularly to be mentored and developed by existing leadership if that people are to grow and be successful in the confirmation of themselves, their vision, ideas and worldviews.

My initial introduction into the values, principles and art of leadership was in four places. First, in the Black church, where a deeply spiritual leadership was developed by a spiritual people. Second for me was during my years in the Boy Scouts of America in the 1950s. Third were those lessons I garnished during my tenure in the United States Army (1960-63). Lastly, what I learned in the previous settings was later reinforced and expanded upon in over thirty-nine years in active Black struggle, African-centered study, teaching, writing, travel and building independent Black institutions. However, the core values of leadership don't change, and are the same that are needed today. Here are the most important ones:

· A sense of family, an understanding of Black culture, enlightened self-pride and democratic ideas and ideals.

- An understanding of racism i.e., white world supremacy in all of its disguises?
- Cleanliness, neatness, order and discipline, discipline and more discipline.
- Education, competency, competition, achievement and creativity.
- Spirituality (personal peace) and charity, a love consciousness for one's people and environment.
- Awareness of the corrupt temptations of money, sex, fame, status and power.
- Respect for self and others.
- A willingness to question authority—especially corrupt authority.
- The ability to keep one's ego in check, understanding the importance of the "I" within the "we."
- Frugality. Careful and economical in taste and lifestyle. Also, environmental consciousness.
- Responsibility for one's acts and decisions.
- The ability to articulate the thoughts of one's self and people clearly, with passion, force and conviction.
- Courage, especially in the face of overwhelming odds and/or evil. Not afraid of new ideas.
- Persistence. Get-up-and-go attitude, stick-to-it-ness. An understanding of personal and political struggle, in a highly complex and changing world.
- Loyalty and duty to self, family, community and spiritual directives.
- Honesty. Honor, trustworthiness, and integrity, beyond question.

· Ownership of self, home, property, business, ideas, and community. The proper use of money and the importance of wealth.

These points only touch the surface of what solid leaders must incorporate into their lives. Ronald Walters and Robert Smith add significantly to this discussion in their book *African American Leadership,* where they state,

> The primary function of Black leadership is to provide the strategic assistance in strengthening the common frame of reference and the common resource base in the Black community in order to help individuals and the group to achieve objectives perceived to be of value. In performing these tasks, leaders must interact in an effective way with followers in a committed maintenance function in the first instance, and in arenas outside of the Black community in the second.

For an oppressed people, liberation struggles create leaders on the fast track of battle and in the fire of quick decisions. Even then, leadership requires a superior knowledge base, active and political fellowship, independent funding sources, clear and agreed upon goals and objectives and a passion for doing that which is good, correct and just. This applies in relationship to individuals as well as our community as a whole.

Continuing their discussion of Black leadership, Walters and Smith add that leadership must understand that,

> The Black community wants to exist within a democratic framework of harmonious social relationships and, as such, desires to be united with the rest of the country in the maintenance and furtherance of democratic procedure and values.

With this in mind, those of you who aspire to lead must always listen to and be among the critical minority. Serious and critical thinking is something that you must do yourselves. It is not a handicap or something that other people do on our behalf. Always remember that few people have eyes for the truth. Most of us have been raised on lies disguised as truths and would not recognize the truth if it were burning at the temples of our minds. Our people need leaders who are thinkers, men and women of scrupulous incorruptness. We do not need "yes people" or "rah rah" enthusiasts who jump and shout to every carefully turned phrase or rhyme.

Remember that when our leaders are not challenged in an honest and non-personal way, they do not grow. History has proven again and again, that it is then that they fall into an arrogance and a selfishness that eventually leads to self-destruction. Black leadership must be spiritually, morally, politically and financially clear and above board. If this is not the case, you can be sure they eventually will be exposed and embarrassed to the point of no return.

Black leadership must understand that they—their lives, finances, personal relations, weaknesses, words, actions, business and cultural associations and families— are under minute by minute scrutiny. In this regard, the question of clean and adequate compensation for human rights leaders is a delicate one. Often, it puts some leaders in a self-righteous mode, allowing them to make monetary and personal decisions that are not in their own best interest or that of our people. Leaders like Marion Barry, Henry Lyons, Louis Farrakhan and Jesse L. Jackson have fallen into this category.

Among my generation's leadership, some have given their lives and that of their families to Black struggle. They see all around them Black economic development that their actions helped ignite, but which they may not gain personal benefit. The reason many of them were called to struggle in the first place is somehow lost because it was not about money, sex, fame or power, but the legitimate needs of Black people. The next generation of Black leaders, must learn from history. Understand that the original charge of Black leadership is negated when personal aspirations become more important than the people and the developmental ideas of the original movement. This sad state of affairs is too often a reality with my generation.

Your generation must be more open to self-criticism. There is an alternative to what we have produced. Don't allow your idealism to be compromised. Don't make private side-deals or play dirty back-door politics; if you do, you will be laughed at and dismissed as no better than the forces you are struggling against. You must be about more than enriching the few on the backs of the many. We as a people cannot effectively negotiate the complicated corridors of power without dedicated leaders who are morally and ethically clean, and appeal to the majority of our people.

In the final analysis, you all, young men and women, must be mini-leaders and understand the political and economic concepts, dangers, rewards and traps of leadership. You live in a new day. For a people who are still growing, it is imperative that we stand as strong and as whole as possible within the larger familihood of the Black world, agreeing not to ever settle for the rising tide of mediocrity, corruption and people disguised as saviors. Inside and outside of our community, Black leadership defines a people just as clearly as their children do—those at Harvard and those locked down in the prisons across this nation. Set grand examples and standards. Do the work others think impossible. And always rise above the limited expectations of others and, yes, yourselves.

# Movements

Young Blacks of my generation were born into Apartheid America. Most of us were very poor. Victimhood as a hat was hanging heavy in the air as we entered adulthood in the 1960s and a great many people were wearing it. I was released from the U.S. Army in August of 1963. In September the murder of four little Black girls in Birmingham, Alabama changed my life forever. I hit the streets of Chicago to be absorbed by the Black Arts, Civil Rights, and Black Power movements of the 1960s and early 1970s. Although these movements have been dismissed by some politicians born with privilege in their oatmeal, these movements saved my life and gave greater meaning and cultural purpose to me, a young developing poet fresh out of the military.

Most of us who participated in these movements realized that they were about real democracy. More specifically, these struggles were about sharing local, state, and federal power, opening up of public facilities to all on an equal basis, empowering the disenfranchised with the vote, recapturing and redefining the Black image in the world mind, equal participation in the educational process by the under-served, enlarging living and working space for people of color, redefining what it means to be a woman in a male-dominant society, and revealing the worldwide destructive powers of racism (white world supremacy).

These Black empowerment movements provided young African Americans of my generation a context for discovering identity and purpose. These movements also provided us with serious proposals for the future. Personally, the movements prevented me from being swallowed by the ever-present lowest common denominator: street culture. Street culture is a culture of containment that too often leads to a dead end. Street culture, as I am using the term, is a counter-force to movement culture. In today's urban reality, it denotes survival at all costs. In contrast, the Black movement existed as extended family, developing a culture that was productive and caring. Involvement in the movement provided me with something to care about that was not insulting to my own personhood. It defined relationships and challenged me to rise above the limited expectations of others and myself. But one of the major contributions was in the arena of ideas.

The 1960s ushered in human rights for Black people. We also took on a new attitude about ourselves. Many of us ceased being Negroes. We became "Black" and "African" and approached life as steps of possibilities. We launched new magazines, publishing companies, independent schools, African-centered churches, financial institutions, electronic media companies and much more—all driven by a new emerging Black middle class with an entrepreneurial spirit.

Much of this was inspired by the older generation. Many of them to this day maintain a dominant impact on our lives. For me there was Malcolm X, who through his vision, words, dignity, actions, commitment and representation of Black manhood gave me a voice and a smile. Margaret and Charles Burroughs, founders of Chicago's DuSable Museum of African American History introduced me to Black institution building and awakened me to the concept of unconditional love of African people. Dudley Randall, my first publisher who as a poet and librarian built Broadside Press out of his home in Detroit, planted in me the seed for my own publishing company, Third World Press. Hoyt W. Fuller, the last managing editor of *Negro Digest/Black World* and *First World* magazines was the first "free" Black intellectual I ever met. His first class education did not separate him from the struggles of the less privileged. Gwendolyn Brooks, the first Black to win a Pulitzer Prize and whose love for Black people and kindness to all was/is infectious, left white publishers to support Black publishers, an act of courage and commitment unparalleled at that time, which influenced me greatly. Finally, there is Barbara Sizemore, an educator extraordinaire who put her world class mind at the service of young people. As a teacher, professor, superintendent of Washington D.C. Schools and university dean, she taught me not to settle for mediocrity, silliness or intellectual corruption from anyone. All of their voices, visions, ideas and creativity live within me today. Their unselfish sharing of time, resources, and money helped nurture me into becoming the man I am today.

Only a people who are short on history and long on consumer culture fail to realize the importance of continuity in our national sruggles. Each generation either continues and builds upon the history and efforts of their foreparents or like ignorant consumers of anything advertised think that they are indeed the first to be enlightened enough to say "no" to insults, disrespect, oppression, inequality and white supremacy.

Young people, especially those of the hip-hop cultural movement, must understand that their movement was created out of a social, political and cultural reality that has existed since the creation of this nation. Young people must study their history as well as the history of all people in order to not make the same mistake that some of us made. More importantly, they must comprehend the enormous task that they face in fighting for a new and just world. They stand on strong and reliable shoulders and if they are aware of such the road that they are paving for themselves and others will have less cracks and holes in it.

I, as a product of Black struggle, see it as a precious responsibility to mentor young men and women, to be there for them in all kinds of capacities: teacher, counselor, employer, example, resource, and on occasion to men to be a fatherly ear. As long as any people are oppressed and locked out there must be opposition to such existence. Remember, we are all accountable and in the final accounting will be held responsible for our actions or non-actions on behalf of the less fortunate of our people and others.

# AFFIRMATIVE ACTION:
## Try Honesty and Fairness

As recently as November 2000, Coca Cola, one of the top beverage companies in the world, was forced by the courts in Atlanta to pay hundreds of millions of dollars to Black workers for past and continued practices of racism. Workers' claims against private and public agencies is not anything unusual in this climate of "blame the victim" politics. The denial that affirmative action, based upon race and sex, is needed continues to slow the real economic and educational development of women and people of color in the United States.

There is very little discussion of white privilege and white male privilege in particular in media or the nation's institutions of higher learning. Do any of us actually believe the reason that whites receive the overwhelming majority of scholarships, government contracts, best-paying-jobs in the nation's top companies, top positions in the nation's major universities and colleges is because of pure merit? Is the reason that the top professional schools—law, medicine and business—are primarily populated with white men (and now white women) due to the innate inferiority of African Americans and other non-white students of color? Will we continue to impair the development of our children by segregating and designating a large segment of our nation as "less" because they need support as a direct result of hundreds of years of legal and illegal discrimination solely based on race?

America does not like to admit to the world that in 2001 there are still tens of millions of poor, homeless, jobless, uneducated and under-educated, misinformed and forgotten people in its cities and rural communities. Their numbers include a substantial population of whites who are used in the battle against affirmative action in an insidious way. In the 1980s and 1990s the rallying cry from angry white men at all economic levels was "reverse discrimination" and the end of race-based preferential treatment. So, not only has race warfare intensified but class warfare has continued to raise its ugly head. One of the most effective strategies of white supremacists has been to pit the white poor against the Black poor. For hundreds of years it has worked to the benefit of all white people, poor, middle-class and the well off. Over the last twenty years or so, prominent Black conservatives have joined hands with their white brothers to denounce, vilify and dismiss affirmative action as an impediment to Black economic and intellectual development.

Three elements are missing from the national debate: (1) white privilege, (2) the laws of accumulation and (3) the question of integrity on the parts of Blacks and whites. We must not forget or rewrite the historical record. White men from Europe stole the country from the indigenous people whom they re-named Indians and re-defined as "savages" and "uncivilized barbarians."

They advanced across the nation committing genocide against the original inhabitants in the name of progress. The concept of Manifest Destiny of European whites backed by superior force and technology eventually conquered the Americas without allotting compensation to the original people on the land. The "founding" of the nation by white male human (a.k.a. slave) owners produced a Constitution and Bill of Rights that benefited and served their status, first and foremost.

The question of the enslavement of millions of Africans was never a serious discussion because the Africans had been reduced to sub-humans and redefined as soulless property to be treated like other ignorant animals. The only importance attached to enslaved Africans was their quality of service to whites of all economic levels. For poor whites or indentured whites, as bad as life was for them, they were always above the "niggers." One may have been dirt poor, without a pot to piss in or shoes to wear, but one's whiteness meant that there were always Black people down on the plantation. Color consciousness emerged as a political and economic weapon used by disenfranchised whites also, primarily men because to a large extent white women did not have political or economic voices.

If we study the historical records (See the works of Carter G. Woodson, John Hope Franklin, Vincent Harding, Chancellor Williams, John H. Clarke, Lerone Bennett Jr., Darlene Clark Hine and others) it is abundantly clear that white men made a world for themselves and their families on the backs of Africans and at the deadly expense of Native people. The rule of white supremacist thought and actions has  freely flourished over the last three centuries.

The sixties brought the rise of civil rights, Black power, white feminists and gay rights activism. The sixties issued a loud call for justice and opportunity for all, especially those people locked out for over three hundred years. All the movements for human rights questioned the rule and dominance of white men. The founding of Black studies and women's studies departments on the nation's college campuses injected other voices into the debates. As a group who highly benefited as a result of affirmative action, some white women began to question their own whiteness and privilege.

Peggy McIntosh adds clarity to this questioning and the extent of the privilege in her essay "White Privilege and Male Privilege," where she writes,

> I have come to see white privilege as an invisible package of unearned assets that I can count on cashing in each day, but about which I was 'meant' to remain oblivious. White privilege is like an invisible weightless knapsack of special provisions, assurances, tools, maps, guides, code books, passports, visas, clothes, compass, emergency gear, and blank checks.

McIntosh seeks a new honesty in questioning her own privilege as a result of being white. Yes, she is highly critical of white male privilege, but as serious scholarship demands she takes a deeper look at how she and other white women benefited. She notes how white men "work from a base of unacknowledged privilege" whereas much of their "oppressiveness was unconscious." White women have unacknowledged privilege too, she admits. She writes of the "frequent charges" from women of color of the racist and oppressive acts from white women they encounter.

> I began to understand why we are justly seen as oppressive, even when we don't see ourselves that way... I began to count the ways in which I enjoy unearned skin privilege and have been conditioned into oblivion about its existence, unable to see that it put me 'ahead' in any way, or put my people ahead, over-rewarding us and yet also paradoxically damaging us, or that it could or should be changed.

Ms. McIntosh's education did not prepare her to see herself and other white women as "oppressors" or "participants in a damaged culture." She was taught, as most of us today, to see herself as an "individual whose moral state depended on her individual moral will." She was taught a distorted history, where slaveholders were not damaged people in a sick and damaged culture. Her edu-

cation taught her that white privilege was a natural benefit of her skin color, more than "class, religion, ethnic
status or geographical location." She details some forty-
six ways on a daily basis that she is privileged for just
being white, such as,

> If I should need to move, I can be pretty
> sure of renting or purchasing housing in an
> area which I can afford and in which I would
> want to live.

> I can go shopping alone most of the time,
> fairly well assured that I will not be followed or
> harassed by store detectives.

> I can turn on the television or open to the
> front page of the paper and see people of my
> race widely and positively represented.

> When I am told about our national her-
> itage or about "civilization," I am shown that
> people of my color made it what it is.

These privileges are so commonplace and totally
interwoven into her day that she says she "forgot each of
the realizations on the list until I wrote it down." For
white men, multiply her list of forty-six by one thousand
and we will begin to understand the magnitude of white
supremacy.

The laws of accumulation are commonsense approaches to understanding white racism's close ties to skin privileges or better yet, insider information for advancement and/or economic gain. It is quite simple. White men built white culture and consciousness into all of their systems, bureaucracies, institutions and governing bodies, infused with the concept of watching each other's back. From white male secret societies to the highly restricted elitist professions of law, medicine, business, education, to the equally restricted manufacturing industry, unions, defense industry and so forth. It doesn't matter whether one is a small business man or CEO of a fortune 1000 company, the inclusion of subsequent generations of white sons (and some daughters) is a forgone fact of life. Obviously in small mom and pop businesses and in medium-sized private or family-owned businesses, one can understand the closed nature of their operations. However, when this culture is duplicated millions of times daily in national, multinational and/or transnational corporations, we have a serious problem. That is why up until Title VII of the Civil Rights Act of 1964 and its amendments the lockout of Blacks and others was part of the blood, soul and fabric of America. With over three hundred years of white male affirmative action, don't tell me that it hasn't been perfected, refined and perfected again.

It goes like this, one's great, great, great-grandfather was a founding father of Harvard University. Therefore a son, daughter or cousin just mentions a name or a code, drops the dollars and he or she is in. We really don't think that George W. Bush was admitted to Yale purely on merit, do we? However, this is not to negate the fact that each year tens of thousands of white students are admitted on merit and seriously compete fairly for the open slots at the nation's best colleges and universities. However, in each industry, union or profession, there are years of accumulated relationships, secrets, information, IOUs and over and under-the-table deals that come due between white men every day that the vast majority of the public know nothing about; from family-owned businesses that have grown and gone public to the tens of thousands of military families that run their sons and daughters through the various military academies.

A few years ago, four white Ivy League MBA graduates started a magazine. In a matter of months they were able to raise over four million dollars on a not so original idea. They got the magazine off the ground, published about six issues and folded. On the other side of the country a Black entrepreneur has been running a small manufacturing company for about twenty-years with thirty employees. The owner, a college graduate, has totally financed his business out of his savings, cash flow of the business and has never missed a payroll, tax payments or filed bankruptcy. In fact he's made a small profit. He can acquire small loans, but has never been able to find the big money so that he can grow and really compete. He is outside of the laws of accumulation— he does not have family, friends, colleagues or any relationship that with a phone call and the right words can get him the millions needed to expand and compete locally, nationally or internationally.

Another example is that of affirmative action at many large and influential law firms. Partners and new associates are given a range of benefits that are not available to most citizens. There is a practice of "red lining" that most banks in urban areas have instituted, arbitrarily denying mortgages to the inhabitants. Many of these same banks have leading law firms representing them. As a part of the sweetheart deal, they offer to the lawyers of the firm no down payment and low interest loans that allow newly made lawyers to buy homes anywhere they desire to live. Again this is one of the thousands of ways relationships or the laws of accumulation work to benefit primarily white people.

Additionaly, on this matter of affirmative action is the issue of integrity. Integrity is the reason I believe that affirmative action is necessary but not for me at this time. Yes, at one time I needed it. I went to college on the GI Bill, affirmative action for military personnel. In building my business and schools, I always experienced cash flow problems, but could not find any real long-term help. In fact, I had to close three bookstores in 1995 because I could not find private investors or banks that believed in the concepts of independent bookstores in the Black community. After thirty-five years of economic struggle and survival, I still have not mastered the game.

However, I mainly say no to affirmative action for

me and my family at the universities and colleges that my sons and daughters attend. Why? Quite simply, my wife and I can afford to pay their way. It would be unethical and hypocritical of us to reach for loopholes and/or trade on relationships to ignore our financial responsibilities that we've struggled and worked for all of our lives. The misuse of affirmative action continues to give ammunition to its critics. Most of all, it continues to keep out the most needed of our people because of the culturally and politically corrupt Black middle-class and upper-class Black folks and white women who think only of themselves. These same Black folks will serve as fronts for white businesses for them to gain minority set-aside contracts, thus hurting the struggling Black businesses that could really develop with this help.

A few years ago an associate of mine told me how he was able to get one of his sons into one of the historical Black colleges and universities on a financial scholarship by going through his contact at the United Negro College Fund. I asked him why he would do such a thing, especially since he and his wife were upper management in their respected companies and obviously could pay the tuition without any difficulty. His response surprised me, "Nobody pays for college these days if they really understand the system." My response to him was, "What system? If you and your wife are not paying his way—we are, I am, the citizens of this country who fought for affirmative action for the most needed of women, Blacks and others are paying. Your son's admission took the seat of someone more deserving of help. For you to use the 'system,' as you describe it, is a betrayal of all we worked and fought for." He was literally taken back at my reaction and of course, he had no legitimate comeback.

I am sure that millions of folks from all walks of life are trying to "get over" and use the "system" for whatever reason. I do feel rather strongly that women, the poor and disadvantaged of this land still need big help. However when we are able to provide for ourselves, we should do it. Cut the umbilical cord to entitlements designed for the truly needy and move on our own. Just as important, we should continue to reach out to those less fortunate and offer our assistance whenever possible.

One last comment on my friend. His son flunked out after one year. The latest is that he is now in a state university and they are paying his tuition. Community and family are important and always the best affirmative action for an individual. When a community can affirm its own action by moving toward financial and cultural independence (neutralizing the effects of racism and power and wealth accumulation among whites) then, and only then, will the poor and others have a fair chance. In the final analysis, affirmative action means to be able to affirm one's actions. Until Blacks folks and others who are systematically locked out have been empowered to do that, help is needed and the beneficiary of such help should not have to continually feel less than human for taking advantage of laws structured to give them a real chance to compete on a clearly unfair playing field.

# REPARATIONS
## The United States'
## Debt Owed to Black People

Debt is owed to African people for centuries of unpaid
    forced labor, suffering,
    death in the tens of millions and the systematic
    seasoning and
    victimization of an entire race of people.

Debt is owed for the willful and brutal separation of
    African people from their
    land, mothers from children, husbands from wives
    and families, children
    from fathers and mothers and a whole people
    from their African land, culture and
    consciousness that defined them and gave them
    substance and
    memory.

Debt is owed for redefining all African people, women,
    men and children as
    slaves and sub-humans not deserving of salvation,
    universal love,
    kindness, human consideration, education and fair
    compensation for all
    forms of labor.
Debt is owed for the designation of African people as

property, three-fifth
humans whose only use is to slave from sun-up to
sun-down, for slave owners, therefore
reduced African people to the category of animals
accorded less care than that of pigs,
sheep, cattle and dogs.

Debt is owed for the inhuman treatment of Africans
forced to slave for the sole
benefit of Europeans, Americans and others for left
over food, clothes
and sleeping space and whose worth and value
was determined by their
production in building wealth for Europe, America
and their people.

Debt is owed for the brutal, ordered, encouraged and
unrelenting rape of
African women by white human (aka slave) traders
and owners, thereby producing a
nation of half-black, half-white children whose
color, status, history and consciousness
branded them forever as bastards, thereby creating
a color, class and cultural
consciousness that to this day continues to rip the
hearts out of African
people maintaining a vicious circle of self-hatred,
self-destruction and denial in them.
Debt is owed for centuries of ruthless, planned and

destructive looting and
whole sale theft of Africa's people, land and miner-
al wealth for the sole
purpose of creating wealth for Europe, the United
States and their
people.

Debt is owed to Black people for centuries of merciless
treatment, mendacious
reordering of the historical record and torturous
psychic damage.

Debt is owed for systematically stealing the cultural
memory from African people, for
the denaturing and renaming them thereby
creating a people unaware of
themselves and whose history and person is now
synonymous with
slavery and slave.

The successful creation of the "Negro" people in the United States is *the* tortuous American tragedy. This white supremacist metaphor started in this land with the ethnic cleansing and genocide of American indigenous people, renamed Indians and/or Native Americans. Thereby, let it be stated forcefully and without doubt or hesitation that the United States was founded and developed on two holocausts, that of the indigenous people and that of the enslaved Africans. Now, today, in this new century and millennium it is documented, confirmed and agreed upon by all thinking and well meaning people that Debt is owed to Native Americans and Black people forced:

To laugh when there is nothing funny,
to smile when they are in pain,
to demean themselves on stage, in film, television and videos,
to dance when their hearts hurt,
to accept delusion as truth,
to lie to their children in the face of contradiction,
to pray to a God that does not look like them,
to pay compounded interest on the wealth they
        created,
to sell their souls for acceptance in a fairy tale,
to mortgage their spirits for another peoples history,
to support white peoples-affirmative action with
        centuries of Black labor and taxes,
to create America's music and be denied the fortunes
        made for others,
to see clearly and act as if they are blind,
to act stupid in the eyes of a fearful rulership,
to say yes when they really mean No!
to go into battle to maim or kill other whites
        and non-whites
        for the benefit of whites.
What does America owe Native American Indians and

Black people?
What is the current worth of America? or
Count the stars in all of the galaxies and multiply in
        dollars by 100 billion,
For a reflective start.

# Vision:
## Young Professionals Must Step Up

If all of the young Black men and women who are now matriculating at the nation's top colleges and universities—from NYU, Yale, Harvard and Columbia to Duke, the University of Chicago, Berkeley, Stanford and the thousands of other colleges, universities, and technical institutions of higher learning—graduate as Black students with a cultural consciousness (Black African Awareness) that guides them to think about positioning the advancement of their own people at the center of their hearts and minds, then we, African Americans, will emerge in the very near future as a collective force unknown to humankind.

*Vision*: Can you imagine producing tens of thousands of Black graduates yearly who are not confused about their identity and who possess a deep and healthy love for themselves individually and their families, country and people collectively? Imagine producing tens of thousands of young people who view themselves as one people within this nation and think, plan and act in the best interest of the collective Black body. Imagine if all these young people fundamentally understood the concept of ownership: ownership of self, family, institutions, businesses, culture and ideas. Imagine if, as a collective body and individually, young Blacks faced the world, not as spineless subjects who bow to every demand of a commercial culture, but as individuals who search for and build upon the life giving, life saving and life affirming ideas of their people and others.

In a survey taken a few years ago, African American people placed eleventh among the leading markets in the world. According to the "World Bank and Target Market News," this position in the world's economic life places Black Americans two-points over its 1997 ranking. As consumers, Blacks in America spend $441 billion annually, following closely behind Spain which was tenth in the rankings. The study points out that African American women "are the leading force in the Black American market," they outspent "any other group in the nation on personal care last year." The U.S. market topped the ranking followed by Japan, Germany, France and the United Kingdom. Italy came in sixth, just above the most populated nation on earth, China. Brazil and Canada closed out the top ten markets. African Americans placed eleventh higher than Korea, the Netherlands and Australia, who were ranked twelfth to fourteenth. We were far ahead of any nation in Africa. Just consider the potential economic strength of African American people if the money we spent stayed in the Black community more than four hours.

This book is a map of possibilities and difficulties. It is a poet's call to young Black men and, of course, young Black women to rise to the occasion and assume control of their lives, our future and the unique opportunities of a changing world. Today's youth movement whether hip-hop or no-hop often seems to run 24/7 without much thought, yet actually requires a great deal of thought, in fact demands serious contemplation on the many guide-posts of daily life that rule and dictate their young lives. To probe and research the emotional, economic, social, cultural, intellectual and political limitations placed upon Black people as a matter of birth requires in each of them a strong personal consititution, deep memory, rigorous discipline and an unquestionable seriousness and honesty. Cultural memory is especially useful in leading them to the necessary truths about themselves as well as their adversaries.

All young Black folks need to be ready, and in a constant rebuilding and sharing mode, they need to understand the importance of family, community and sharing. We cannot and should not hide or minimize our many failures or defeats, nor should we overplay our many successes. The critical factor is to learn from both. We need cold but warm eyes, closed but loving hearts, a war-like but peaceful spirit and a soul that will accommodate all of these contradictions. This only speaks to the complexity of the human condition.

What I am suggesting is a higher and more responsible level of self-determination, which at its core requires one to be self-loving, self-critical and honest to the bone. Such personal and collective movement demands an accurate historical memory that takes into account the idealistic passion of young people which will incorporate a well thought out rationale for their actions. Young people must understand in no uncertain terms that self-determination is possible and that one's words and actions are fundamentally inseparable from integrity, progress and, of course, bright tomorrows for all if one is serious.

Self-determination must be fundamental in our thoughts and actions. Two examples of people who have maintained a deep cultural and spiritual consciousness while fighting much of the world as they built a life for themselves are the Jewish people and Mormons. Jews number about six million in the United States and about thirteen million worldwide with Israel and New York as their major population centers. The Mormons who number about eleven million worldwide are based in Salt Lake City, Utah and actually rule the state: politically, culturally and economically. These two groups are worth serious examination for several reasons.

1. They are extremely successful in a world that has not been kind to them;
2. Spiritually and philosophically they are at "odds" with the mainstream in terms of religion and many cultural practices;
3. They define themselves as "one" people and move collectively as they allow and encourage individual devleopment;
4. The Jews, more so than the Mormons, encourage

debate, criticism and analysis. However, both peoples view education and serious study as critical and necessary for development;

5. They tax themselves, take care of themselves and control the financial institutions that ultimately fund their worldview and movements;

6. They are as serious as a first love about themselves, their ideas and their future; and

7. They are predominantly white people who are able to move unnoticed in and out of critical arenas for the benefit of individuals and the collective.

I reference Jewish people and Mormons because each group functions in its own trillion dollar economy that is a part of the world's economy. Their legislators, business people, educators, professionals and skilled people and others are not only dedicated to the building of the United States but equally committed to their own religious and secular communities.

Black people in the United States number over thirty-five million, some believe closer to forty million. Let's state for debate that about twenty million adult African Americans are citizens of the United States. If twenty million Black folks invested one dollar a week into a common fund at the end of one year it would equal one billion, forty million dollars ($1,040,000.000) plus interest. After just two years, this money invested in "safe" five per cent interest earning accounts would equal about two billion, one hundred and eighty four million dollars give or take a few million. Is this possible? I say, Yes.

*Vision*: We, as Black people, need a "Black American Congress" where we meet at least twice a year to forge ahead on a national and international agenda that will work tirelessly to improve the lot of African Americans and by extension, that too of America and Africa.

A gathering of Black folk, mainly non-traditional leadership and fellowship. We desperately need to move beyond the old-style civil rights and Black power leadership who for the most part are only accountable to their families, friends, co-workers, peers and lovers. I feel that the groups that need to take the lead are the Black MBAs, Black lawyers, bankers, CPAs and Blacks in corporate America who are often called on individually for money but never as a collective body. The many Black professional organizations like the National Association of Black Social Workers as well as national associations of Black doctors, nurses, psychologists, fraternal organizations and others.

I do acknowledge a few drawbacks with this proposal:

1. Who would Black people trust to administer such a fund?
2. How would representation for a "Black Congress" be chosen?

Just as with any people, trust is earned and in all

Black communities there are men and women who already are working in sensitive positions that require deep financial knowledge and trust. In order to determine who should attend the National Black Congress, we have professional event planners and organizers who can start seriously thinking about this and circulate their findings and suggestions to the Black nation. The major point is that young men and women must take the lead on this and make it happen—it's their time.

In conjunction with this Congress, by the year 2004, we should begin to organize an annual African American World Youth Summit where Black youth of America meet among themselves, with some guidelines and financial help from their parents and elders, to really look at the future of Black people nationally and internationally. And, finally, we need a truly democratic Black Think Tank that the great social scientist Nathan Hare visualized over a generation ago. A Think Tank populated by and financed by Black people with no political, cultural or financial agenda other than the development and betterment of Black people at home and abroad. With the intellectual talent that we are producing each year, to do anything less is a profound comment both on the failure of Black struggle over the last fifty years as well as the intellectual and cultural soundness of the young Black people we are producing.

# Memoirs of a
# Poet/Activist

In many ways, my life has been dedicated to the development and liberation of my family and Black people, and myself.  Liberation to many is considered a 1960s word, but I believe in it.  This has never been a small commitment to me. I am as serious about this as first love. For the last thirty-nine years, the single most compelling question that has energized me is, how do we take ownership of our lives?

Much of my work has been about trying to put my life and Black life into context. Why else would I do what I do? Why spend thirty-four years building a publishing company? Why spend thirty years building schools for children? When you look at communities that are self-empowered, you find men and women who have devoted their lives to building institutions that further develop their concept of themselves. These self-empowered people do not have to go out into never-never land and try to find something that they can identify with, that is given to them by people who do not even like them. I am not even getting into racism. I am saying a great many people—white and others—just do not like Black folk.

One of the tragedies of Black life in America (and even in the diaspora) is that too many people of African ancestry never acquire insight into their own existence. We just do not know who we are. This confusion about identity and source is at the core of our ignorance. Thus, the question of education has always been very important to me. The education I received in the Black community was entirely different in content and context from that of whites growing up in the 1950s. Not only was my training not a challenge, it was discouraging. The major pieces of information I absorbed after twelve years of public education was that I was a problem, inferior, un-educable, and—guess what?—a victim. One of the things about being a victim is that you begin to see the world through the eyes of a victim. As a victim, you can never be a winner. On the contrary, you wallow in victimization. The only cure for victimization is to question it, define it, put it in its historical and cultural context and move toward clear and practical solutions that can be shared with others. To that end, let me share one of my experiences from which I've learned.

I will never forget how hard my mother worked to make ends meet for my sister and me. Our material lives were impoverished. I grew up around pimps and whores slammin' Cadillac doors. We did not have a television, record player, car, telephone or much food. We were lucky when the lights and the gas were on at the same time. We acquired much of our clothing from second-hand stores, and I learned to work the streets very early.

But my life began to change when I was introduced to other worlds. One year, on my birthday, my mother took me to a five-and-dime store to buy me a gift. She bought me a blue plastic airplane with blue wheels, a blue propeller, and a blue string on the front of the plane so that I could take it home and roll it on the linoleum floor. I was happy to get that airplane.

The following week, she took my sister and I to Dearborn, Michigan, where she occasionally did domestic day work. This was back in the day when many of our mothers cleaned up white folks' homes for a living. Dearborn was where the men who ran the automobile industry lived. I quickly noticed that they lived differently. There were no five-and-dime stores in Dearborn at that time. There were craft shops. There were hobby shops where white mothers and fathers brought their children airplanes in boxes.

In the boxes were wooden parts and directions for assembling and gluing small airplanes. It might take a day or two, or a week or so, for the son generally, and sometimes the daughter, to assemble a plane. If he or she could not do it by himself or herself, the child would ask the father to sit down and help put it together. And guess what? After the plane was put together, the little girl or boy did not roll it on the floor. He or she took it outside and it flew.

In this small slice of life, two different types of consciousnesses are being developed. In my case and that of other poor youth, we would buy the plane already assembled, take it home, and hope that it rolled on the floor like a car or a truck—but it was an airplane! In Dearborn, the family would invest in a learning toy that the child would put together. Through this process, the child learned work ethics, science, and math principles.

As a result, the plane would fly. I was learning to be a consumer who depended upon others to build the plane for me. The child in Dearborn worked on his plane, made an investment, and through this labor and brain power produced a plane that flew. Translating that into the larger world, I was being taught to buy things and to use my body from the neck down, while the white upper-class boy was being taught very early to prepare himself to build things, to run things, and to use his body from the neck up. Two different worlds. My world depended upon others and on working for others. His world consisted of controlling, running, making things, and having other people work with and someday for him. From that day on I began to look at the world with a new set of eyes and consciously started using my head rather than my heart to make choices and decisions.

When I was thirteen, and I will never forget this, my mother asked me to go to the Detroit Public Library to check out *Black Boy*, by Richard Wright, and I refused to go. I had bought into the concept that Black was bad. I didn't want to deal with anything that was Black. The self-hatred that occupied my mind, my body, and my soul simply prohibited me from going to a white library in 1955 to request from a white librarian a book by a Black author, especially one with "Black" in the title. I, like millions of other young Blacks at the time, was a product of a white educational system that, at best, taught me to read and respect the literary, creative, scientific, technological, and commercial achievements of others. No one actually told me, "You should hate yourself." However, the images, symbols, products, creations, promotions, and authorities of white America all very subtly, and often quite openly, taught me white supremacy. Along with white supremacy, these social forces taught me to hate myself. The white supremacist philosophy of life was unconsciously reinforced in Black homes, in Black churches, clubs, schools, and communities throughout the nation. Therefore, my refusal to check out *Black Boy* was in keeping with the culture that twenty-four hours a day denied me and my people the fundamental rights and privileges of citizens and refused to admit that we were even human beings. Few articulated it in popular culture at the time, but we lived in apartheid USA. Even still, *Black Boy* somehow attached itself to my mother's mind and would not let go. Finally, I went to the library, found the book on the shelf, clutched it to my chest, walked to a vacant spot in the library, sat down, and began to read the book that would profoundly change my life.

For the first time in my life, I was reading words developed into ideas that were not insulting to my own personhood. Richard Wright's experiences were mine, even though we were separated by geography. I read close to half the book before the library closed. I checked *Black Boy* out of the library, hurried home, went into the room that I shared with my sister and read the book well into the night.

Upon completing *Black Boy* the next morning, I literally overnight had become a different type of questioner in school and at home. I had not changed totally, but the foundation had been planted deeply. I became more concerned about the shape of things around me. I also read Wright's *Native Son, Uncle Tom's Children*, and *Twelve Million Black Voices*. Wright painted pictures with words that connected me to the real me. I could relate to Bigger Thomas because his fears exposed an internal rage for the same things that I had experienced. Layers of ignorance were removed just by my mind being opened to a world that included me as a whole person. Wright entered my young, impressionable life at the right time.

My mother died in 1959. After her funeral, I took the Greyhound bus to Chicago, where I stayed with my father and stepmother for a while. Then I rented a room at the YMCA. I completed high school in Chicago and ended up in St. Louis, Missouri in the United States Army, at the age of eighteen. The military was the poor boys' answer to unemployment. The Army changed my life.

On the way to Fort Leonard Wood, Missouri, for basic training, I was reading Paul Robeson's *Here I Stand*. We arrived at boot camp, and the white, mid-thirty-something drill sergeant ordered us off the bus. We were about two hundred men—three Blacks and one hundred ninety-seven whites. The Black men had all joined voluntarily, but most of the white men had been drafted. This was 1960 and the Army was practicing integration.

As I stepped off the bus, the white drill sergeant spotted Paul Robeson's large, smiling Black face on my book.

"What's your Negro mind doing reading that Black Communist?" he barked into my face, snatching the book from my hands.

It was the first time I had heard a double negative used so creatively. Many thoughts ran through my mind. For one thing, I was questioning my own sanity for having joined the military. Another thought that came to mind was something I learned from my earlier reading of John Oliver Killens' *And Then We Heard The Thunder*, a powerful and telling book about World War II. I learned from Killens the importance of using one's time wisely and of never speaking from the top of one's head in anger when one is outnumbered.

"All of you women up against the bus," the drill sergeant ordered.

There were not any women there. The whole deprogramming had started. We jumped up against the bus. He held my book, Paul Robeson's words, over his head and commenced to tear the pages out and give one to each of the recruits to be used, according to his orders, for toilet paper. I stood, lips closed, cold and shaking with fear, anger, and loneliness while the drill sergeant destroyed my copy of Robeson's work. At that moment, I decided upon four propositions that would stay with me for the rest of my life.

First, I would never, never again apologize for being Black. I am who I am, and I realized then that if Black literature had taught me anything, it clarified for me that I was a man of African ancestry in America serving time in the U.S. Army, rather than the U.S. prison system.

Second, I would never again put myself in a cultural or intellectual setting where people outside of my culture knew more about me that I knew about myself. This meant that I had to go on the offensive and put myself on a re-education program to prepare myself culturally and intellectually as an African in America, as a Black man.

Third, I was in the U.S. Army because I was Black, poor, and ignorant of the forces that controlled my life and the lives of other men, Black and white, with whom I was to train. These forces were social, economic, and political, and I needed accurate information on all of them. So while many of the other brothers in my platoon searched for fun, I visited libraries. They could not understand why I chose to be alone with books. The reason was that I found a new set of friends, uncritical friends, in literature. I was like a sponge. Reading became as important as water, food, and even sometimes sisters.

And fourth, if ideas were that powerful—able to cause such a reaction—then I decided that I was going into the idea business. For that drill sergeant to act so violently against a book that contained ideas he probably

did not even understand was frightening. He was reacting to the image and the idea of Paul Robeson that had
been created by white monied, political, and mass media
power brokers. Totally absent from his perspective was
the reality that Paul Robeson was one of our great, great
heroes!

From that day on, I have been on a mission to
understand the world and to be among the progressive
women and men who want to change it for the benefit of
the majority who occupy it. My two years and ten months
in the military were essentially my undergraduate education. During that time, I studied the history, economics,
political science, literature, of course, poetry, and culture of Black people. I was reading E. Franklin Frazier,
Langston Hughes, Claude McKay, Jean Toomer, C.L.R.
James, John O. Killens, J. A. Rodgers, James Baldwin and
others. One of the most influential writers to impact on
my thinking then was W.E.B. DuBois, who had by then
already articulated the problems of the twentieth century. As I studied his work, I began to see possibilities for
myself. Given the color complex in our community,
DuBois, a fair-skinned brother as myself who devoted his
life to the uncompromising development and liberation
of Black people, revealed possibility for myself in our
struggle. He was both activist and political theorist and in
all of his work he advocated the need to reconstruct the
Black mind.

I came out of the military in August of 1963 with the
plan to go to college in September under the GI Bill. But

something happened in September that changed the course of my life. Four little girls were murdered in the bombing of a church in Birmingham. For a young man like me who had been trained by the Army to be a killer, the question was, do I join these racist people who are killing our children, or do I begin to move in a direction of liberation? That is where I went, and I think that is where I am still today. And that is where I will be until I die. It is as simple as that.

The revisionist history of the 1960s is incorrect. The activist struggles of that decade changed America for the best. I entered adulthood in the sixties via the U.S. Army and into the streets of Chicago to be absorbed by the Black Arts, the Civil Rights and the Black Power movements. Whereas in my formative years I had been subtly taught to hate myself (and in the military to kill people who looked like me), the movements which encompassed all the 1960s and part of the 1970s gave me greater meaning and greater cultural purpose.

The Black movements afforded young African Americans of that period a context for discovering identity and purpose. The movements also supplied us with serious proposals for the future. The movements prevented many young women and men of our time from being swallowed by street culture. The movements existed as an extended family creating a culture that was productive and caring. The movements gave us as young people something to care about that was not insulting to our own personhood. They defined relationships and challenged us to defend and to define our own limited resources.

A major contribution of these movements was in the arena of ideas. There were few Black or African American studies programs before these movements. In those early days it was very clear to most of us that if we wanted to move toward consciousness, we had to find whatever books there were available on Black history and culture, carry them in our back pockets our knapsacks, and swap, exchange, or share them with each other. That is how we aquired this knowledge. There were few courses on African American literature or on Black writers in most institutions of higher learning. We got it from the streets. For the first time in the lives of many of us, we were confronted with ethical, moral, spiritual, political, historical, and economic questions and dilemmas. Through our day-to-day activities, we were forced to think at another level about the United States and the world. Often our lives depended upon the quality of our thinking and our decisions. Such critical thinking at such a young age matured many of us. We began to see that our struggles were deeply attached to international realities and liberation struggles in other parts of the world. We were reading the works of Carter G. Woodson, Frantz Fanon, Amilcar Cabral, E. Franklin Frazier, Gwendolyn Brooks, Margaret Walker, Richard Wright, John Oliver Killens, Kwame Nkrumah, Julius Nyerere, Marcus Garvey and many others. One could go on and on. It was great. We loved and cared for each other. The Black movements that existed then do not exist today. This is not to suggest that there are no movements today. The profound difference is that there is now no national Black political movement of any consequence.

Even during the 1960s and 1970s, there were many streams, but there was only one river. There existed a national consensus on broadly defined goals and objectives. Whether one worked for the NAACP, CORE, SNCC, SCLC, the Urban League, the Nation of Islam, the Black Panther Party, US organization, or the Congress of African People, one had a connection, a force, a greater purpose and definition that was beyond one's personal geography.

In keeping with our time, a group of us came together in the mid-1960s and began to ask, "What can we do?" It was in the spirit of the time that I decided I was going to be a poet/writer. I made a promise to myself that any money I made from writing would be used to start a publishing company. And with my first $400, I started Third World Press in my basement apartment. The apartment was about the size of a large table, and I shared it with other animals and a mimeograph machine.

When I started Third World Press in 1967, there were only four Black publishing companies and ten Black bookstores in the entire country. For over thirty-five years Third World Press has been in the forefront of progressive Black publishing. This is a long story that involves many, many people. I was not trained as a businessman and had to learn on the job. I've made mistakes that have cost me a great deal of money and at times dampened my spirit, but my heart and mind have always been focused on doing that which is right.

Book publishing is not a business that is traditionally in our community. I learned a great deal from Dudley Randall, the founder and publisher of Broadside Press in Detroit, Michigan. Mr. Randall was the first publisher to take a chance with my books and with TWP. I tried, just as he had, to give other Black writers a chance.

As a poet, I have always been concerned about publishing poetry. However, seldom can a Black publishing company stay alive with just a poetry line. In the 1970s I began to publish in all areas; fiction, non-fiction, drama and children's books. Over the last thirty-four years we have published some of the major writers and thinkers of this or any century from Amiri Baraka, Gwendolyn Brooks, John Henrik Clarke, Pearl Cleage, Derrick Bell, Cheikh A. Diop, and Mari Evans to George Kent, Useni Eugene Perkins, Kalamu ya Salaam, Sonia Sanchez, Askia Toure, Frances Cress Welsing, Chancellor Williams, Bobby E. Wright and many others.

In 1969, a group of us, including my future wife, came together, and agreed to start a school. We all came out of the Chicago public school system not knowing much about ourselves and our people, so we were sure that we could do at least as well as, if not better than, most public schools. We started the New Concept Development Center and Institute of Positive Education in a storefront. Then we moved to two storefronts, and after that we bought a building about ten blocks from where we had started. We stayed there for about twenty years, until we outgrew both. In 1993, we moved into a larger facility nearby. We bought a half-block, a former Catholic parish. This was over a million dollar investment which put us in another category of Black struggle.

It has not been easy. We are in the middle of the Black community in Chicago. We do not have big benefactors. We do not have large pockets. We do have people like Wesley Snipes, Walter Mosley, Ossie Davis, Ruby Dee, Avery Brooks, Chester and Ann Grundy, Calvin Jones, Malachi Favors, Murray DePillars, Gwendolyn Brooks, alongside a community of many others supporting our schools.

My advice to you, young brothers, is that you have got to start thinking about building Black independent institutions now. Stop thinking about what Fortune 500 company you are going to give your lives to. You may indeed have to go there to gain experience, and to learn some of the secrets of economic development and wealth accumulation. But you cannot abandon our communities. There must be a middle ground where our skills and talents are also shared with Black people in a meaningful way, if we are to develop.

When we examine well-defined communities, we see that they and the people who control them have institutions that reflect their ideas and their values. As young people, you have to dream. You have to think the impossible is indeed possible. If we are seriously considering our liberation, we must begin to think about developing institutions that reflect us, serve us, and provide us with new progressive leadership as we move into the new millennium.

Institutional development is not easy. However, in order to effectively fight institutional control over Black folks we need committed institutions, controlled and funded by us at every level of human activity.

# You Will Recognize Your Brothers

You will recognize your brothers
by the way they act and move throughout the world.
there will be a strange force about them,
there will be unspoken answers in them.
this will be obvious not only to you but to many.
the confidence they have in themselves and in
their people will be evident in their quiet saneness.
the way they relate to women will be
clean, complimentary, responsible,
with honesty and as partners.
the way they relate to children will be
strong and soft, full of positive direction and as example.
the way they relate to men
will be that of questioning our position in this world,
will be one of planning for movement and change,
will be one of working for their people,
will be one of gaining and maintaining trust within the
culture.
these men at first will seem strange and unusual but
this will not be the case for long.
they will train others and the discipline they display
will be a way of life for many.
they know that this is difficult
but this is the life that they have chosen
for themselves, for us, for life:
they will be the examples,
they will be the answers,

they will be the first line builders,
they will be the creators,
they will be the first to give up the weakening pleasures,
they will be the first to share love, resources and vision,
they will be the workers,
they will be the scholars,
they will be the providers,
they will be the historians,
they will be the coaches,
they will be the doctors, lawyers, farmers, clergy
and all that is needed for development and growth.
you will recognize these brothers
and
they will not betray you.

# Epilogue: Hard Truths
## September 11, 2001 and
## Respecting the Idea of America

I do not wear an American flag on my collar, nor is there a flag on my car or on a window in my home. For those who proudly display the flag I feel that it is their right to do so, just as it is my right not to join them. I am a veteran, volunteering and serving in the United States Army between October 1960 and August 1963, discharged honorably and early to attend college on the G.I. Bill of Rights. The military was my way out of debilitating poverty and I will never speak ill of it. However, I am wise enough to not send my sons when the options of a first class university is there for them (two of them attended Northwestern University). On the road to becoming a poet, I have learned to love America. Coming to this conforming feeling was not easy or expected. On my many journeys, if I've picked up anything, it is to question authority in America.

For me the attack on the World Trade Center was personal because my daughter's workplace is a short block and a half away. She was en route to work when the first plane hit. Just before the second plane exploded she was on the phone talking to me with tears clearly interrupting her speech.

I was literally shaking in Chicago as I told her to immediately take the safest route out of town and go home. Because roads were blocked, traffic was jammed, and public transportation was not accessible, she had to walk. She was twenty-five and ended up taking off her cute pumps to walk in her bare feet from lower Manhattan to Brooklyn where she lives. Like most citizens of the nation I was enraged and angry. And while viewing man-made mass destruction on innocent people in New York, the one city in the United States that best represents the possibilities of true multi-culturalism, I too was ready to fight. However, for me the critical question was not how 9/11 happened, but why?

As a poet, educator, publisher and cultural activist I have had the privilege to travel and interact with people in nearly every state in the United States. I have served on the faculty of major universities in Illinois, New York, Washington D.C., Ohio, Maryland and Iowa. Between 1970 and 1978, I commuted by air each week between Chicago and Washington D.C. to teach at Howard University. In the early eighties, I drove each week between Chicago and Iowa City for two and a half years to teach and earn a graduate degree at the University of Iowa. These commutes and other travels nationally and internationally over the last three decades have enlarged me in unexpected ways. The United States is a very large and beautiful country. Its population is reasonably well-educated and is highly diverse—racially, ethnically, religiously, economically and culturally. This reality gives me cause for hope.

This hope has helped me to escape the trap of

accepting simple generalizations about racial and ethnic groups and narrow assumptions about their political positions. Serving in the United States Army as a very young man, taught me that close quarter living, serious open-minded study, daily conversation and interaction with people of other cultures can do wonders in eradicating stereotypes and racial and ethnic pigeonholing.

My work over the last thirty-nine years has been confined almost exclusively to the African American community, the same community where I live, work and build institutions. As a result, I have few white, Asian, Latino American or Native American friends or associates. I am quite aware that there are literally tens of millions "good and well" meaning people of all cultures doing progressive political and cultural work every day. I say this because it is very easy to take the negative acts of some people and assign them to all people of a particular ethnic group, race or culture. But the plain truth is that we are all individuals. And it is best to accept or reject people based upon their individual talents, gifts, intellect, character and politics. America's many cultural and ethnic groups share the English language, public education, popular culture, mass media, and the powerful and effective acculturation into Western civilization and culture. In essence, if we are honest, we are more alike than many would admit.

I wrote in my book *Enemies: The Clash of Races* (1978), that I loved America but loathe what America had done to me, my people and other non-white citizens of this country. I still stand on these words. We must never forget that America's "democracy" was built on the destruction of the hearts, minds, souls, spirits, bodies and holocausts of the Native peoples and Africans. This fact is not taught in the nation's elementary, and secondary schools, or universities—although it remains the secret behind the enormous economic success of the United States. The nation's inability to honestly come to terms with its own bloodied past with public debate, acknowledgment and restitution remains at the heart of the centuries old racial divide. The sophistication of today's oppression of Native peoples, Black, Latino and poor people is much more insidious, institutionalized and thereby excused by media, politicians and corporate America as something of the past.

At the same time, we must acknowledge the vast changes in voting rights, employment, housing patterns, political representation, legal and health care structures, access to secondary and higher education and the creation of a large, yet fragile Black middle class. None of this would have come about if not for the many Black struggles over the last one hundred years that forced the powers that be to accept their own laws, and not discriminate against people purely on racial or ethnic differences.

Our struggles here for full citizenship, equality, fair access to all the opportunities afforded white citizens remains at the core of progressive Black struggle. Our right to be politically active is fundamentally what democracy is about. This is no small right. My work of writing, teaching, editing, publishing, traveling to speak, organizing conferences and workshops and other cultural and political activities that I and other like-minded people of all cultures are involved in, in the United States could not be done in Afghanistan, China, Nigeria, Haiti, Iraq, Liberia, Uganda, Sierra Leone, Libya, Colombia, Kuwait and most of the member nations of the United Nations.

In the early seventies, I often thought of migrating to Africa. However, after visits to many African nations, discussions with African Americans who have migrated and returned, and my non-romantic assessment of the African continent economically, politically and culturally, I decided against it. I realized after a great deal of soul-searching and private and public debate that I could help Africa and its people (us) more by working hard to be a success here and like the Irish, the Jewish and other ethnic groups reach out to my people abroad. This decision remains critical in my thinking and actions today.

My focus in this book is to let young, and not so young, brothers know that we do have realistic options in America. It is my responsibility to communicate to you that our ancestors' centuries old bloodied fight for human, economic and political rights in the United States has not been in vain. Our people, against unrealistic odds, have taken the dirt, crumbs, scorn and ideas of America and secured a tangible future for generations of Blacks to compete and make their own statements about success and attainment.

Yes, there is still much more to do. I have tried to give some insight into the politics of that work in this book. However, many (not all) African Americans have more freedoms, prosperity, liberties and possibilities in the United States than Black people any place in the world today. Of course, those of our people in this category are still a fragile minority. As contradictory, inconsistent, racist and unfair as America continues to be, it still is a nation that does afford a chance, an opportunity to those who are intelligent, organized and strong, focused and bold, serious, hard working, and lucky enough to make their statements heard.

I can state unequivocally that my publishing company, Third World Press, publishes only the books that I, and its editorial staff agree upon. Yes, there has been political and economic pressure on us to not publish certain books. However, these pressures did not directly come from the United States government. The two African centered schools I co-founded, New Concept pre-school and the Betty Shabazz International Charter School likewise continue to exist without open opposition from the government. For twenty-one years myself along with other conscious and committed young brothers and sisters operated multiple book stores in Chicago and only closed them in 1995 because of serious competition from the super chain bookstores. But that, in the United States, I and millions of others have been able to fight for our space even in often difficult political and economic structures is a comment on the possibilities of this country. That I have never had the economic resources to really compete with the major or mid-stream publishing companies is also a comment on the work that still needs to be accomplished in this nation.

A central part of the responsibillity of an informed citizen is to question our government, especially its foreign policy which helped to create an Osama bin Laden, Al Qaeda, corrupt monarchs in Saudi Arabia and key nations all over Africa. As the nation grieves and buries its dead we must not allow ourselves to just automatically buy into the answers from our government.

The larger question from us must be why, after investing over thirty billion dollars of our taxes a year, with few questions asked, is it that the Federal Bureau of Investigation (FBI), Central Intelligence Agency (CIA), the National Security Council and the Defense Department didn't have a clue to what was happening? And, now a week after 9/11 there is a call from those agencies for people who speak the indigenous languages of Afghanistan and others. Could racism be the reason for a lilly white, angel bread security force who can't currently find its way out of a computer program. Most certainly these people could not get back in the field where the real dirty work of human intelligence is being done. Thirty billion dollars for what? This is the type of gross incompetence and racism that Black folk and others have to deal with daily.

So, young brothers, I want you and young people of all cultures to know that the idea of America can become a reality, can become the visionary eye in the center of the storm, the organic seed growing young fertile minds, can be the clean water purifying the polluted ideas of old men fearful of change, can take democracy from the monied few to the concerned majority if we believe in its sacred potential and the potential of the twenty-first century's coming majority of Black, Brown and locked out white people. The best of you must rise. This eminent majority must not have the white supremacist mindset of the founding patriarch or the "superior" souls of the current rulership. Those among this coming majority must be nurtured and educated in the essential tenets of democracy. Many of you have tasted the debilitating effects of being denied your birth rights. So when the time comes for you to lead, you must be able to look your children in their eyes and state with firmness and clarity that you do believe in democracy and fairness for all people and not just the monied few and numerical majority. We too stand and will fight for the historical ideas of the Declaration of Independece, United States Constitution and its Bill of Rights. Finally, we must take ownership of ourselves, our families, communities and this vast and beautiful land. In doing so we will be making the most profound statement on our citizenship, and in the words of the great poet Langston Hughes, "We too Sing America."

## SELECTED BIBLIOGRAPHY and
## SUGGESTED READING LIST

Allen, James. *Without Sanctuary: Lynching Photography in America*. Santa Fe: Twin Palms Publishers, 2000.

Abu-Jamal, Mumia. *All Things Censored,* edited by Noelle Hanrahan. New York: Seven Stories Press, 2000.

Abu-Jamal, Mumia. *Death Blossoms: Reflections from a Prisoner of Conscience*. Farmington: Plough Publishing House, 1997.

Achebe, Chinua. *Home and Exile*, Oxford: Oxford University Press, 2000.

Aesop. *Fables of Aesop*. Translated by S.A. Handford. New York: Penquin Books, 1954.

Aldridge, Delores P. *Focusing: Black Male-Female Relationships*. Chicago: Third World Press, 1991

Alexie, Sherman. *One Stick Song*. New York: Hanging Loose Press, 2000.

Amnesty International. *The Case of Mumia Abu-Jamal: A Life in the Balance*. New York: Seven Stories Press, 2000.

Anderson, S.E. and Tony Medina. *In Defense of Mumia*. New York: Writers & Readers Publishing Inc., 1996.

Ani, Marimba. *Yurugu: An African Centered Critique of European Cultural Thought*. Trenton: Africa World Press, 1994.

Arnold, Johann Christoph. *Endangered: Your Child in a Hostile World*. Farmington: Plough Publishing House, 2000.

Asante, Molefi Kete and Abu S. Abarry, Editors. *African Intellectual Heritage: A Book of Sources*. Philadelphia: Temple University Press, 1996.

Bandele, Asha. *The Prisoner's Wife: A Memoir*. New York: Scribner, 1999.

Banks, William M. *Black Intellectuals: Race and Responsibility in American Life*. New York: W.W. Norton, 1996.

Baraka, Amiri. *Wise, Why's, Y's*. Chicago: Third World Press, 1995.

Barras, Jonetta Rose. *Whatever Happened to Daddy's Little Girl?*. New York: The Ballantine Publishing Group, 2000.

BeGala, Paul. *"Is Our Children Learning?" The Case Against George W. Bush*. New York: Simon & Schuster, 2000.

Bell-Fialkoff, Andrew. *Ethnic Cleansing*. New York: St. Martin's Griffin, 1999.

Bennett Jr., Lerone. *Forced Into Glory: Abraham Lincoln's White Dress*. Chicago: Johnson Publishing Company, 2000.

Benston, Kimberly W. *Performing Blackness: Enactments of African-American Modernism*. London: Routledge, 2000.

Berry, Wendell. *The Hidden Wound*. Boston: Houghton Mifflin Co., 1970
*What Are People For?* New York: North Point Press, 1990.

*Sex, Economy, Freedom and Community*. New York: Pantheon Books, 1992.
*Another Turn of the Crank*. Washington, DC: CounterPoint, 1999.
*Life Is A Miracle*. Washington, DC: CounterPoint, 2000.

Boyd, Herb and Robert L. Allen. *Brotherman: The Odyssey of Black Men in America — An Anthology*. New York: Ballantine Books, 1999.

Brooks, Gwendolyn. *Primer for Blacks*. Chicago: Third World Press, 1980.

Browder, Anthony T. *Survival Strategies for Africans in America*. Washington, D.C.: The Institute of Karmic Guidance, 1996.

Burns, Khephra and Susan L. Taylor. Editors, *Confirmation: The Spiritual Wisdom That Has Shaped Our Lives*. New York: Anchor Books, 1997.

Burroughs, Tony *Black Roots*. New York: Simon & Schuster, 2001.

Byrd, Rudolph P. and Beverly Guy-Sheftall, Editors. *Traps: African American Men on Gender and Sexuality*. Bloomington: Indiana University Press, 2001.

Carruthers, Jacob H. *Intellectual Warfare*. Chicago: Third World Press.

Carter, Stephen L. *Integrity*. New York: Harper Perennial, 1996.

Chesler, Phyllis. *Letters to A Young Feminist*. New York: Four Walls Eight Windows, 1997.

Chomsky, Noam. *Pirates and Emperors*. New York: Claremont Research & Publications, 1986.

*Year 501: The Conquest Continues*. Boston: South End Press, 1993.

*Rethinking Camelot: JFK, Vietnam War, and U.S. Political Culture*. Boston: South End Press, 1993.

*The Common Good*. Interview by David Barsamian. Berkeley: Odonian Press, 1998.

*What Uncle Sam Really Wants*. Tucson: Odinian

Press, 1999.

*The Prosperous Few and the Restless Many.* Interviewed by David Barsamian. Tucson: Odinian Press, 1999.

*Profit Over People.* New York: Seven Stories Press, 1999.

*Rogue States.* Cambridge: South End Press, 2000.

Coles, Robert. *The Secular Mind.* Princeton: Princeton University Press, 1999.

Collins, Chuck and Felice Yeskel. *Economic Apartheid in America.* New York: The New Press, 2000.

Collins, Patricia Hill. *Black Feminist Thought,* second edition. London: Routledge, 2000.

Curry, George E. Editor, *The Affirmative Action Debate.* Reading: Addison-Wesley Publishing Co., Inc., 1996

Dahl, Robert A. *On Democracy.* New York: Yale University Press, 2000.

Darrow, Clarence. *Crime & Criminals.* Chicago: Charles H. Kerr Publishing Company, 2000.

Davis, Ossie and Ruby Dee. *With Ossie & Ruby.* New York: William Morrow & Co, 1998.

Delbanco, Andres. *Required Reading.* New York: Farrar, Straus and Giroux, 1997.

Denton, Sally and Roger Morris. *The Money and the Power: The Making of Las Vegas and its Hold on America 1947-2000.* New York: Alfred A. Knopf, 2001.

Diawara, Manthia. *In Search of Africa.* Cambridge: Harvard University Press, 1998.

Dowd, Siobhan. Editor, *This Prison Where I Live: The Pen Anthology of Imprisoned Writers.* London:

Cassell, 1996.

DuBois, W.E.B. *Black Reconstruction in America: 1860-1880.* New York: World Publishing Co., 1964.

Evans, Mari. *How We Speak.* Chicago: Third World Press, (in press) 2002.

Fanon, Frantz. *The Wretched of the Earth.* New York: Grove Press, Inc., 1963.

Feagin, Joe R. *Racist America: Roots, Current Realities, and Future Reparations.* New York: Routledge, 2000.

Frady, Marshall. *Jesse: the Life and Pilgrimage of Jesse Jackson.* New York: Random House, 1996.

Frank, Stanley D. *The Evelyn Wood Seven-Day Reading and Learning Program.* New York: Barnes & Noble Books, 1990.

Frankl, Viktor E. Man's *Search For Meaning.* New York: Washington Square Press, 1984.
*Recollections: Viktor E. Frankl An Autobiography.* Translated by Joseph and Judith Fabry. Cambridge: Persey, 2000.

Fussell, Paul. *Class: A Guide Through the American Status System.* New York: Summit Books, 1983.

Goldberg, David Theo. *Racist Culture.* Oxford: Blackwell, 1993.

Goldberg, J.J. *Jewish Power.* Reading: Addison-Wesley Publishing Company, Inc., 1996.

Golden, Marita. *Saving Our Sons.* New York: Anchor Books, 1995.

Gourevitch, Philip. *We Wish To Inform You That Tomorrow We Will Be Killed With Our Families: Stories From Rwanda.* New York: Faraar Straus and Giroux, 1998.

Greene, Robert. *The 48 Laws of Power*. New York: Penguin, 1998.

Gross, Jan T. *Neighbors: The Destruction of the Jewish Community in Jedwabne, Poland*. Princeton: Princeton University Press, 2001.

Guy-Sheftall, Beverly. Editor. *Words of Fire: An Anthology of African American Feminist Thoughts*. New York: The new Press, 1995.

Hanh, Thilh Nhat and Daniel Berrigan. *The Raft Is Not The Shore*. New York: Orbis Books, 2001.

Harrison, L. E. and Huntington, S.P. Editors, *Culture Matters*. New York: Basic Books, 2000.

Haskins, James and Hugh F. Butts, M.D. *Psychology of Black Language*. New York: Hippocrene Bible, 1973.

Hawken, Paul and Amory Lovins, L. Hunter Lovins. *Natural Capitalism*. Boston: Little, Brown & Co., 1999.

Henderson, David R., *The Joy of Freedom*. New York: Prentice Hall, 2002.

Herman, Edwards S. and Noam Chomsky. *Manufacturing Consent*. New York: Pantheon Books, 1998.

Hitchens, Christopher. *No One Left to Lie To: The Triangulations of William Jefferson Clinton*. London: Verso, 1999.

*The Trial of Henry Kissinger*. London, Verso, 2001.

hooks, bell. *Outlaw Culture*. London: Routledge, 1994. *Salvation: Black People and Love*. New York: William Morrow, 2001.

*Where We Stand*. London: Routledge, 2000.

Hutchinson, Earl Ofari. *The Assassination of the Black Male Image*. New York: Touchstone, 1996.

Ivins, Molly and Lou DuBois. *Shrub: The Stort but Happy Political Life of George W. Bush*. New York, Random House, 2000.

*Nothin' but Good Times Ahead*. New York: Random House, 1993.

James, Joy. *Transcending the Talented Tenth*. London: Routledge, 1997.


Jett, Joseph and Sabra Chartrand. *Black and White on Wall Street*. New York: Morrow, 1999.

Johnson, Chalmers. *Blowback: The Costs and Consequences of American Empire*. New York: Henry Holt and Co., 2000.

Jordan, June. *Technical Difficulties*. New York: Pantheon Books, 1992.

Karenga, Maulana. *Introduction to Black Studies*. (New Edition.) Los Angeles: University of Sankore Press, 2001.

Kitwana, Bakari. *The Hip-Hop Generation*. New York: Basic Books, 2002.

Korten, David C. *When Corporations Rule the World*. West Hartford: Kumarian Press, Inc., and San Francisco: Bennett-Koehler Publishing, Inc., 1996.

Lapham, Lewis H. *Money and Class in America*. New York: Weidenfelf & Nicolson, 1988.

Lerner, Gerda. *Why History Matters*. New York: Oxford University Press, 1997.

Loewen, James W. *Lies My Teacher Told Me*. New York: The New Press, 1995.

Maass, Peter. *Love Thy Neighbor: A Story of War.* New York: Vintage Books, 1996.

Madhubuti, Haki R. *Black Men: Obsolete, Single, Dangerous?* Chicago: Third World Press, 1990.

Madhubuti, Haki and Safisha Madhubuti. *African-Centered Education.* Chicago: Third World Press, 1994.

Malveaux, Julianne. *Wall Street, Main Street and the Side Street.* Los Angeles: Pines One Publications, 1999.

Maraniss, David. *The Clinton Enigma.* New York: Simon & Schuster, 1998.

Mauer, Marc. *Race to Incarcerate: The Sentencing Project.* New York: The New Press, 1999

Medina, T. Bashir, S.A. and Lansana, Q.N. *Role Call: A Generational Anthology of Social and Political Black Literature.* Chicago: Third World Press, 2002.

Mills, Charles W. *Blackness Visible: Essays on Philosophy and Race.* Ithaca: Cornell University Press, 1998.

Morrison, Toni. *Playing in the Dark: Whiteness and the Literary Imagination.* Cambridge: Harvard University Press, 1992.

Mosley, Walter and Manthia Diawara, Clyde Taylor, Regina Austin. *Black Genius: African American Solutions to African American Problems.* New York: W.W. Norton, 1999.

Mosley, Walter. *Workin' On The Chain Gang.* New York: The Ballantine Publishing Group, 2000.

Nelson, Jill. *Volunteer Slavery: My Authentic Negro Experience*. Chicago: The Noble Press, Inc. 1993.

Parenti, Christian. *Lockdown America: Police and Prisons in the Age of Crisis*. London: Verso, 1999.

Parenti, Michael. *Dirty Truths*. San Francisco: City Lights Books, 1996.

    *American Besieged*. San Francisco. City Lights Books, 1998.

    *History as Mystery*. San Francisco: City Lights Books, 1999.

Pierce-Baker, Charlotte. *Surviving The Silence: Black Women's Stories of Rape*.

Peletier, Leonard. *Prison Writings: My Life Sing Sun Dance*, edited by Harvey Arden. New York: St. Martin's Press, 1999.

Parents, Michael. *History as Mystery*. San Francisco: City Lights Books, 1999.

Pollitt, Katha. *Subject to Debate*. New York: The Modern Library, 2001.

Prashad, ViJay. *The Karma of Brown Folk*. Minneapolis: University of Minnesota Press, 2000.

Price, Frederick K.C. *Race, Religion & Racism, vol. 2*. Los Angeles: Faith One Publishing, 1982.

Price, Reynolds. *Feasting the Heart*. New York: A Touchstone Book, 2000.

Quindlen, Anna. *A Short Guide to a Happy Life*. New York: Random House, 2000.

Rich, Adrienne, *Arts of the Possible*. New York: W.W. Norton & Company, 2001.

Reed, Ishmael. *The Reed Reader*. New York: Basic Books, 2000.

    Ed. *Multi America*. New York: Viking, 1997.

Reed, Jr., Adolph. *Class Notes*. New York: The New Press, 2000.

Reid, Frank M. *Restoring The House of God*. Shippensburg: Treasure House, 2000.

Reynolds, Barbara. *Jesse Jackson: the Man, the Movement, the Myth*. Washington: Associated Publishers, 1975.

Roy, Arundhati. *The Cost of Living*. New York: The Modern Library, 1999.

Ruiz, Don Miguel. *The Four Agreements*. San Rafael: Amber-Allen Publishing, 1997.

Said, Edward W. *Representations of the Intellectual*. New York: Pantheon Books, 1994.

Schlosser, Eric: *Fast Food Nation*. Boston: Houghton Mifflin Co., 2001.

Schneider, Bart. Editor, *Race: An Anthology in the First Person*. New York: Crown Trade Paperback, 1997.

Silbiger, Steven. *The Jewish Phenomenon*. Atlanta: Longstreet Press, 2000.

Smiley, Tavis. *Doing What's Right*. New York: Doubleday, 2000.
Ed., *How to Make Black America Better*. New York: Doubleday, 2001.

Smith, Robert C. *We Have No Leaders*. Albany: State University of New York, 1996.

South End Press Collective. *Talking About a Revolution: Interviews*. Cambridge, 1998.

Staples, Brent. Parallel Time. New York: Perennial, 2000.

Terkel, Studs. *Talking to Myself*. New York: Pantheon Books, 1997.

Thurman, Howard. *A Strange Freedom*, edited by Walter

Fluker and Catherine Tumber. Boston: Beacon Press, 1998.

Timmerman, Kenneth R. *Shakedown: Exposing the Real Jesse Jackson*. Washington, DC, 2002.

Trumpbour, John. Editor, *How Harvard Rules*. Boston: South End Press, 1989.

Unger, Roberto Mangabeira and Cornel West. *The Future of America Progressivism*. Boston: Beacon, 1998.

Vidal, Gore. *The Decline and Fall of the American Empire* Berkeley: Odonian Press, 1992.

Wade-Gayles, Gloria. *Pushed Back to Strength: A Black Woman's Journey Home*. Boston: Beacon Press, 1993.

Walters, Ronald W. and Robert C. Smith. *African American Leadership*. Albany: State University of New York, 1999.

White, Vilbert L. *Inside the Nation of Islam*. Gainesville: University Press of Florida, 2001.

Wideman, John Edgar. *Hoop Roots*. Boston: Houghton Miffin Company, 2001.

Williams, Daniel R. *Executing Justice: An Inside Account of the Case of Mumia Abu-Jamal*. New York: St. Martin's Press, 2001.

Williams, Patricia J. *Seeing A Color-Blind Future: The Paradox of Race*. New York: The Noonday Press, 1997.

Willis, Ellen. *Don't Think, Smile: Notes on a Decode of Denial*. Boston: Beacon Press, 1999.

Wills, Garry. *A Necessary Evil*. New York: Simon & Schuster, 1999.

Winbush, Raymond A. *The Warrior Method*. New York: Amisted, 2001.

West, Cornel and Kelvin Shawn Sealey. *Restoring Hope: Conversations on the Future of Black America.* Boston: Beacon Press, 1997.

Yancy, George. Editor, *African-American Philosopher.* London: Routledge, 1998.

Zinn, Howard. A Peoples History of the United States *1492-Present: 20th Anniversary Edition.* New York: Harper Collins Publishers, 1999.

*On War.* New York: Seven Stories Press, 2001.

# Haki R. Madhubuti

Poet, educator, essayist, editor, founder and publisher of Third World Press (1967), co-founder of the Institute of Postive Education (1969), New Concept School (1972) and Betty Shabazz International Charter School (1998). He is the Distinguished University

Professor and the founder and Director Emeritus of the Gwendolyn Brooks Center at Chicago State University. Professor Madhubuti is co-founder and chairman of the board of the International Literary Hall of Fame for Writers of African Descent. He is the recipient of many awards for his poetry and cultural work, such as National Endowment for the Arts and National Endowment for the Humanities, American Book Award, Gwendolyn Brooks Distinguished Poets Award, Illinois Art Council award and others. He has published twenty-five books including the bestselling *Don't Cry, Scream!* (1969), *Black Men: Obsolete, Single, Dangerous?* (1990), *Claiming Earth: Race, Rage, Rape, Redemption* (1994), *Groundwork: New and Selected Poems from 1966-1996* (1996), and *HeartLove: Wedding and Love Poems* (1998). His latest book is *Tough Notes, A Healing Call: Creating Exceptional Black Men* (2002). He has given keynote addresses, lectures and poetry readings at thousands of colleges, universities and community institutions worldwide. In August of 2001, he was appointed Director of Chicago State University's newly created Master of Fine Arts in Creative Writing Program.

For engagements contact (773) 651-0700.